The Pastor's Wedding Manual

The PASTOR'S WEDDING MANUAL

Jim Henry

BROADMAN
& HOLMAN
PUBLISHERS
Nashville, Tennessee

© Copyright • Broadman Press
   All Rights Reserved
ISBN-13: 978-0-8054-2313-6
ISBN-10: 0-8054-2313-3
Dewey Decimal Classification: 252.1
Subject Heading: WEDDINGS
Library of Congress Catalog Number: 84-17594
Printed in the United States of America

Library of Congress Cataloging in Publication Data

Henry, Jim, 1937-
   The pastor's wedding manual.

   1. Marriage service—Handbooks, manuals, etc.
2. Weddings—Handbooks, manuals, etc. I. Title.
BV199.M3H46   1985   265'.5   84-17594
ISBN 0-8054-2313-3

06 07 08 09   19 18

Dedicated in gratitude to God:

For every couple I've been privileged to "tie the knot" for through the years;

For their aspirations to make their wedding a celebration of the love of Jesus Christ;

For their commitment to biblical principles for godly homes;

For their vows to keep their vows until death does part them.

Contents

Before They Say "I Do"

It was early in my second pastorate. A fine couple, active in the church, asked me to officiate at their wedding. So far as I knew, there was nothing to hinder me. From all reports everything was in order, and I was pleased that they had asked me as the new pastor to share in their wedding.

Prior to the wedding I probably did not spend more than ten minutes with them, unfortunately. I took too much for granted. At the wedding they were the picture of marital bliss. For several months it seemed they had a picture-perfect marriage. Then one day he did not come home from work. He pulled a disappearing act and simply walked away from his brokenhearted wife and relatively new bride. It was a shock to her and to me.

In a way, I felt partially responsible. I kept asking myself, *What if*... I had checked into his background more, discussed the principles of a Christian home, shared his conversion and commitment to Christ, talked over the wedding ceremony and its components, had them read some helpful books on building a strong home, understanding their temperaments, sexual knowledge, and the challenges their marriage would face.

I did none of the above. I simply served as the "marrying parson" believing they would "live happily ever after." After all, they were adults, older than I, and they should have known what they wanted in the person with whom they would share the rest of their lives. My naiveté was glaringly exposed in this traumatic incident.

But I learned from it. I determined that in the future, to the best of my ability, I would do everything possible to tie a "tight knot" with every couple I married. I recognized that I could not be wholly responsible for a failing marriage, but I certainly did not desire to be even partially responsible. Next to the conversion experience, marriage is probably the most significant commitment we make in our lifetime. Since what happens to the home reflects on communities, churches, nations, and businesses; since children from a marital union are impacted by their home environment— as a minister of the gospel I have a golden opportunity to influence the direction of that new home in its formative stages.

From that moment on, I made the counseling and the wedding event a priority in my ministry.

I read, studied, listened, and inhaled all I could about weddings, marriage, and the home. I then viewed the biblical teachings in a clearer light. As the years have rolled by, I have come to certain basic convictions and commitments I trust have been helpful to those I have tied together in marriage.

In over twenty years as a pastor, I have officiated at several hundred wedding ceremonies. To the best available knowledge, I cannot name over a dozen of those marriages that have ended in the divorce court. I do not take credit for that, but I am convinced that the time the staff and I devote to a couple, the strong demands and expectations our church has for godly homes, and the instruction we provide in one-on-one sharing, small-group study, and from the pulpit have undergirded those couples in building a lasting marriage. I also feel strongly that the wedding ceremony itself and all of the attendant proceedings have added a binding dimension to the marital ties.

The wedding ceremonies here have a strong biblical emphasis. You will recognize that none of these services are "five-minute specials." I see the wedding ceremony as one of those superb "teachable moments," not only for the couple but for the attendants, the family, and the friends who attend. In fact, through the wedding we have been able to reach at a later date many of these people for Christ and His church. The touchstone was the wedding ceremony. The Holy Spirit used it to convey certain eternal truths to which members of the wedding party were open at that particularly sensitive moment.

I have also made several other observations about a Christian wedding ceremony. First, the higher demands we have made on the couples concerning counseling, a Christian worship service, and a time limit (*discussed later in this chapter*) have not lessened the demand for our services—but increased them! When we put on our agenda the priorities God places high on His, we can expect blessing. I thought some of our expectations would run people away; instead, they seem to be invisible magnets drawing people from all walks of life.

Second, we have observed a high level of appreciation for the time, effort, and energy that I personally, the church, other staff members, and laity have put into their wedding and pre-wedding plans.

Third, the weddings have become more Christ-centered and worshipful. There is a sense of expectancy, a feeling that the living Christ is indeed involved with what is going on. Many couples even ask me to make sure that the gospel is included in my remarks, that some of their unsaved family members or friends can hear the way to eternal life.

My fervent prayer is that these introductory pages will be instructive, informative, and inspiring to those who read them and use this book in future years. I do not consider myself the ultimate authority on premarital counseling, marriage, and wedding ceremonies. No two ministers will perceive and do everything in the same manner, but we have found and practiced some things which have stood the test of the years and proven workable and helpful. I trust you will face the same situation, that the plowing of your life into those who sought you for assistance in marriage will cause them to remember you as one of the strong links in forging an enduring chain of love in a joyous Christian home.

The Premarital Interview

I suppose the first question to be asked is why I require a premarital interview. I've found some couples who expect it and desire it, but some are shocked when informed I want to talk with them before consenting to marry them. It is particularly offensive to those who think of the minister and the church as an addendum, a "necessary evil," or someone you are supposed to include because that makes it "legal," or it is a cultural custom. The interview is basic to all else that follows. Here are some of the reasons:

It enables you to get to know the couple in a much deeper relationship. Thus, when they stand at the altar, they see you as a trusted friend and vice versa.

It prevents those who want you to marry them on the spur of the moment from taking advantage of your compassionate spirit and demanding your services because you are a minister. When you explain you have a policy requiring everyone you marry to have an interview with you, and you have a minimum time requirement of three months' notice, it removes pressure and enables you to deal meaningfully with those who are serious about marriage.

(*I use three months for advance notice; you may use a time limit suiting you. I have found the three months give time for the counseling, preparation for the marriage, and clearing the church calendar. In fact, I prefer six months. The reason? If there are serious problems that unfold, there is time to correct them or even delay the wedding. It gives you ample opportunity for positive input concerning the rehearsal, the wedding ceremony, and the building of an enduring union.*)

It gives you opportunity to provide the couple

with specific information concerning the spiritual, emotional, and physical aspects of their marriage.

It enables you to work out the details for the wedding and answer any questions they may have relative to the service, rehearsal, time, and place.

It provides the privilege to ascertain their personal commitment to Jesus Christ and His lordship in their lives. I have had the joy of leading many prospective brides and grooms to Christ in or after the interview session. I have often found it reveals what a person is not willing to commit or does not believe. This usually comes as a shock to the other party, but it is an eye-opener, a confrontation which can lead to salvation, conviction, or understanding of biblical principles of which they may have been ignorant. It can be painful or pleasant, but handled carefully, worthwhile for all involved.

The interview is preeminently important. Failure at this point can be detrimental to all concerned. Participation in a well-planned and prayed-over interview is one of the great blessings of the pastor's ministry. How many sessions should you plan for? I believe that is determined by the emphasis you as a minister place upon the Christian wedding ceremony and marriage. Every conscientious minister has hectic schedules, but this should have top priority. Through the years, until recently, I had three sessions lasting for thirty to forty-five minutes. In my present pastorate, I have one session of forty-five minutes to one hour. If I make a commitment to officiate at the wedding, the couple is referred to a six-session premarital counseling course our church offers on Sunday nights year-round. This gives the couple six hours of teaching conducted by another minister, plus the reading of books, listening to tapes, and completion of a workbook.

The question inevitably comes: What if they cannot come on Sunday night because of schedule conflicts, or one of them has to be away in college or service? We offer some alternatives. If there will be some weekends when they can be in town, a minister will meet with them for at least two sessions other than the original interview. If that is impossible, tapes, books, and the workbook are required to be read, listened to, and completed.

The majority is appreciative of these expectations, and I cannot recall anyone who has been unable to fulfill the requirements. In fact, our willingness to share in the wedding is predicated not only on the interview but also the attendance in the classes and the fulfilling of the requirements. If the couple is not willing to spend time seriously considering their wedding and marriage, they disqualify themselves as far as I am concerned.

The Structure of the Interview

I cannot offer you a stereotype of what you should do or say, but I can share a few of the subjects we deal with and the questions we ask. They are to the point and sometimes seem rather blunt. I have discovered that no one has the luxury of beating around the bush. Specific questions tend to receive specific answers. I have discovered that in some cases we delve into areas where the couple has never probed. It opens a new world to their own communication process; it enables them to think through or rethink some preconceived notions; it allows their discussions with me and each other to reach a much deeper level.

Let me briefly share the aesthetics, room setup, and personal preparation I bring to the interview.

I make sure it is private. The couple must know that their personal remarks are being made to you alone, and that their confidences will not be betrayed. Therefore, the room should be out of earshot of everyone else, and if possible, out of eyesight, too!

Second, I try to set them at ease as much as possible. Friendliness, warmth, and a hearty welcome help to set nervous marriage prospects at ease. I begin with chitchat, maybe telling them something funny or challenging that has happened to me that day; I inquire how their day is going. Before we move into the questions, I pause and lead in a word of prayer, asking God's leadership and blessing on our session.

Third, I arrange the room so they are seated together, facing me. This gives them more togetherness plus the encouragement they need as they face this uncertain time with a man they may have observed from the pulpit more than any other place!

Fourth, I offer them some orange juice or a cup of coffee as we begin. They usually refuse it, but that act of concern helps to establish rapport and a sense of caring.

Fifth, I try not to assume an authoritative stance. If I begin with that attitude, I may find myself "preaching" and the couple trapped listeners. The interview is an inducement for them to talk! That does not mean I do not make observations or give guidance, but I do all I can to get the couple to open up and share. It is good for them individually, it is good for them to hear what the other is thinking, and it gives me insights I can draw on later in the interview.

Sixth, I find that forty-five minutes to one hour is more than enough time for one interview. Longer sessions can degenerate into repetition and wasted time. At the conclusion of our share time, I ask the couple to join hands with me, and I lead in a prayer for them, their families, their wedding, and their future home.

Last, but not least, be prayerful. Eternal matters are at stake. Future joy and directions, family happiness, children, and even salvation may be determined by this critical time. It may be that these two are really not compatible for marriage and need to discover that before they make a drastic mistake. (*We have had several couples to decide that, break their engagement, and start over in another direction.*)

I recognize that this potential home will be a blessing or a curse to the couple, their family, any children they may have, and ultimately their community and our nation. I cannot haphazardly approach this hour. All eternity and time is wrapped up in it. I lean heavily on the Holy Spirit to guide me and them as we share.

Questions and Aspects of the Wedding and Marriage to Discuss

During the course of the years I have assimilated questions from several sources to pose to the couple in our session. I do not ask all of them, but I will list several of them for you to choose from in premarital counseling sessions.

The Spiritual

1. How long have you known each other?
2. How did you meet?
3. What attracted you to the other partner?
4. Were you reared in a Christian home?
5. What church background? (*If different, I ask them if they have considered belonging to the same church and settling the issue before marriage.*)
6. Have you made a personal commitment to Jesus Christ as your Savior and Lord? Tell me about it.
7. Do you understand Christian marriage: (*Eph. 5; 1 Pet. 3:1-7, submission to each other?*)
8. Is there any impediment to this marriage? (*Divorce, pregnancy, family disapproval, etc. If any, what has been done about it?*)
9. What place does the Lord's church play in your life? Now and in the future?
10. What are you doing, and what will you do to encourage mutual growth in the Lord?
11. Do you pray together now? If not, will you begin to share in this spiritual experience?
12. Will you plan a wedding ceremony that will exalt the Lord Jesus Christ?

The Practical

1. What is your future spouse's strongest point? Weakest?
2. Do you get along with your prospective in-laws?
3. Do you know what your total income will be?
4. Have you planned a tentative budget?
5. Who will be president, and who will be secretary-treasurer in your home? (*Or who handles the checkbook? Will you have separate accounts?*)
6. Do you have the same interests?
7. How do you like her friends? His?
8. How do you settle disagreements?
9. Are either of you overdependent on parents?
10. Is there anything in marriage which you fear?
11. Have you knowledge of any disease, particularly hereditary, which might affect your future?
12. Do you have any mutual long-range goals?
13. Do you have any outstanding debts? What are your feelings about debts?
14. Where will you live? In close proximity to in-laws?
15. How will marriage make you a better person?
16. Do you have a sense of humor?

17. Can you discuss your deepest thoughts and concerns with your partner?
18. Do you really listen to each other?
19. How do you treat your parents?
20. Do you know the state/county laws concerning blood tests, marriage license? Who will bring the license to church on your wedding day?

The Physical

1. Do you know the difference between sex and love?
2. Have you read any books on the physical aspects of marriage? Or marriage in general?
3. What if you discover one partner is more demanding sexually than the other?
4. Do you both want children? When? How many?
5. Will you make a commitment from the time of this interview until you are one in Christ in Christian marriage to be sexually pure toward one another?
6. If you have already become intimate, will you confess it to the Lord, ask His forgiveness and strength to be pure until you are married?

Before I move to the procedural section, which deals with rehearsal, music, type of vows, etc., I want to include our six-session format for premarital counseling. In the words of my associate pastor, "The alarming rate of marital miss instead of marital bliss" caused us to have a burden for a more effective teaching and counseling approach to marriage preparation.

We believe that it is incumbent upon the church to introduce biblical principles of marriage, for parents to be role models for marriage, and for children and youth to have instruction and example at home and church. We seek to permeate our education programs, pulpit ministry, youth retreats, and extra activities such as seminars with a strong emphasis on the Christian home, family, and Christian behavior in dating.

This seminar takes place after the initial interview with the minister. It is led by a minister on our staff (*if no associate, the pastor could handle it*) assisted by an exemplary couple from our laity. The format:

Session 1—"The Biblical Principles of Marriage," (*roles of husband/wife; purpose and direction*)

Session 2—"Taylor-Johnson Temperament Analysis" (*expectations in marriage*)

Session 3—"Love, the Foundation for Marriage" (*30-minute videotape on characteristics of* *love; eros/philos/agape life-style; Jesus, the Source of love, 20-minute dialogue*)

Session 4—"Problems, Pitfalls, and Panic" (*Crisis areas of anger, jealousy, finances, etc.*)

Session 5—"Communication in Marriage" (*40-minute videotape on principles of communication, problems of communication, the vows; 20-minute dialogue on same*)

Session 6—"The Expanded Family: In-laws and 'Outlaws.'" (*Living as God's family, establishing devotions, relative heat and humidity*)

The minister or counselor meets the couple at a later time for discussion of the results of the Taylor-Johnson Temperament Analysis and any other evaluations or adjustments.

The normal programming of most local churches offers several natural opportunities to assist the total family and home emphasis: Bible studies in Sunday School, small-group studies, family seminars in the church or area-wide opportunities featuring men and women who are excellent communicators on the subject, family devotion and prayer emphasis, Christian Home Week, youth and family retreats, a film series, publications with strong family emphases, a pulpit series by the pastor, and distribution of tapes and books on marital health.

We even have periodic weeks in the church calendar year where we urge our people to stay home or do something with their families. We clear our calendar of church activities except for the regular services. It has been most effective, and we don't hear any complaints!

The Procedural

Here are some of the practical aspects of the rehearsal and the wedding. The minister should have a form for the couple to fill out. Included in this chapter is a type of form you might find helpful to you as the officiating minister and to the person in charge of the rehearsal.

In my last two pastorates the Lord has provided our church with gifted women to direct the rehearsal. They understand my usual procedures and perform a tremendous service in this ministry. They give a cohesiveness to what we are doing. They know the facilities, the available church properties (*candelabra, kneeling altar, etc.*), and other personnel involved. Practically, it also frees me on that night for a date with my wife or family.

If such a person is available in your church (*It could also be a man; one large church has a custodian who does this effectively and has for years!*), I would strongly urge you to train her and then release her to this ministry. Her title could be wedding director or wedding consultant.

Rehearsal Information

DEAR FRIENDS: Your wedding day is a very important day in your life. The actual wedding, whether very simple or extremely ornate, is important. You should prayerfully plan it so as to glorify God. One of the members of our fellowship will be in charge of the rehearsal. In order that she can be of the most help to you, please fill out the following form.

This form should be completed and returned to the church office at least one week before the rehearsal.

Bride's name:_____ Phone no._____
Groom's name:_____ Phone no._____
Date & Time of Rehearsal:_____
Date & Time of Wedding:_____
Please give the names of the following:
    1.   Organist:_____
    2.   Soloist:_____
    3.   Any other musicians:_____

    4.   Person who will direct your wedding:

    5.   Maid or Matron of Honor:_____
    6.   Bridesmaids:

        (1)_____ (4)_____
        (2)_____ (5)_____
        (3)_____ (6)_____

7. Flower Girl:_____
8. Any other female participants:_____
9. Best Man:_____
10. Ushers: *Groomsmen*

        (1)_____ (4)_____
        (2)_____ (5)_____
        (3)_____ (6)_____

11. Ring Bearer:_____
12. Any other male participants: _____

It is important that all participants in the wedding be present at the rehearsal. It is not advisable, however, for too many people who are not participating in the wedding to attend the rehearsal. This is sometimes distracting and time-consuming.

How will your attendants enter the church?

    a. Ushers together and bridesmaids single file
_____

    b. Ushers and bridesmaids paired together
_____

    c. Other (please explain)_____

Will they use:

    (a) Center aisle_____
    (b) Side aisle_____
    (c) Other (please explain)_____

Will you use the kneeler?

Will you use the cross?

Will you use the three-candle ceremony?

Will you have printed programs?

Will you use an aisle carpet?

(If the flower girl is to drop petals, you must have an aisle carpet.)

Give name of usher who will seat bride's mother:

Give name of usher who will seat groom's mother:

Give names of two ushers who will light candles:

Give names of two ushers who will unroll aisle carpet:

How many songs will you have?

Where will they be in the ceremony?

Where will the soloist stand?

Do you plan to stand facing the choir loft or facing the congregation? Or a combination of the two?

Please list or describe anything else you plan to do that will be a variation from the traditional wedding.

The Wedding Ceremony Questionnaire

This is to be completed and turned in to the church office at least one week before the rehearsal. It will be used at the rehearsal and then given to the minister performing the ceremony.

Name of bride and groom:

Date of wedding:
Do you want the traditional ceremony?
Do you want the traditional ceremony with some
variation?
If so, please explain:

Will you write any personal or special vows?
If so, are these to be used instead of or in addition
to the regular vows?
Do you plan to say anything to each other?
Do you plan to say a word of thanks to your
parents?
Do you plan to have the three-candle ceremony?
Please briefly give the order to be followed for the
service, being sure to include songs, etc.:

If you are planning anything special or different,
please describe briefly.

A most essential part of the wedding ceremony
is the music. It can make all of the difference in
the spiritual experience of the service. Do not take
it for granted. I have attended weddings where
everything from "The Exodus" to "This Ol'
House" was played. We have sought as a church
to emphasize tremendous Christian music and to
eliminate secular music. If we cannot, we seek to
move the secular music to the very first part of the
service or to the reception. The following are some

of the things we seek to share with the prospective couple. We find that most couples have given little thought in using music in the most uplifting and meaningful way:

The words are most important.
During the ceremony it is advisable to choose selections that are a maximum of one to one-and-one-half minutes in length. Before the processional any length is suitable.
At several points during the ceremony, music can be used to enhance the service:

(a) When the bride reaches the front, as an introduction to the ceremony: a short prayer hymn, Scripture song, or hymn about the meaning of Christian love.

(b) At the conclusion of the ring ceremony: any of the types mentioned above are proper, or there are a few wedding selections recently composed that have words specifically about the rings and their meaning.

(c) During a prayer time: this is especially effective if the couple kneels at a kneeling bench or prayer altar. (*Remind them to pick a short one. You can get uncomfortable quickly when kneeling in your wedding finery.*)

(d) If the unity candle ceremony is used, there

are compositions that have words directly related to this.

(*e*) Choose the spots carefully. Too much music can detract.

Choose the musicians for your wedding prayerfully. They should understand the purpose of a Christian marriage. They should be fully sympathetic to the minister's direction and submissive to his leadership.

If the church has a minister of music or other church staff musicians, they should be consulted. Instrumentalists should be totally familiar with the instrument they will play. (*Don't bring in Aunt Suzie or Cousin Amy who has never been in your church until your wedding day!*)

Choosing the Vows

It seems that in recent years, Christian couples have expressed a desire to make their vows more meaningful. For some it means to write all or part of them. For others, it means a return to the traditional vows which for a period fell into disuse.

Through the years I have sought to make every wedding ceremony different. I have mixed traditional and contemporary; I have added new Scriptures, poems, or illustrations. I always say a personal word about the couple: something related to their church life, their families, or some mutual experience I have been privileged to share as their pastor. This adds a personal touch, depth, and warmth that would not ordinarily be present —also a freshness that everyone seems to appreciate.

I believe you will find these ceremonies usable as a whole or in parts. You can use them interchangeably; that is the charge or wedding purpose in one and the vows in another. Your personal knowledge of the couple will help you choose the one that is most appropriate. I strongly encourage the couple to write some of their own vows, have a personal word to say to their parents, lead in prayer, or even share in a testimony. I ask them for any Scripture, poem, or vows they would like to add and to feel free about such.

The Rehearsal Itself

The rehearsal can be a grand occasion or a nightmare. If you participate in the rehearsal, the following may be helpful.

Have your service already chosen, as well as the vows, etc. Any change made between rehearsal and wedding can be a disaster.

Begin on time. The word will soon leak out that you start when you say you are going to (*and it will make everyone happier because you will eat dinner sooner and everyone will reach home quicker*).

Try to secure someone to direct the rehearsal, preferably someone who knows you and the church. It will save everyone plenty of wear and tear. The tension at this point is reaching a high level and a firm, decisive, and steady director can help everyone.

Begin with a word of prayer. This helps to set the proper tone for the next twenty-four hours. It is especially meaningful for those who are not Christians. They begin to see another side of the event besides the usual lightheartedness, and it probably reduces the tendency for some to be risqué in their remarks. This does not mean that you do not laugh or have a good time, but it does tilt the event Godward, and that is how it ought to be.

Go through everything at least twice. Be sure that in the rehearsal you prompt the couple about anything that could come up and how it is to be handled. (*Someone drops a ring: What do we do?*) They need to be assured that you are in control and will guide them safely through until the final amen! This takes much pressure off them and relieves some of their fears. For most of them it is the first and, hopefully, the last time they will do this, and they are inexperienced. Confidence in your leadership breeds confidence in the couple and assists them in really participating in the worship experience on their wedding day.

The Wedding

I try to arrive early enough to go through my notes, the sermonette, the personal remarks, the vows, and the order of service to be sure it is fresh in my mind and heart, then I put on my robe.

(*I started wearing a robe several years ago for many reasons. It saves me time and energy of searching for the right clothes for each wedding. I also find the black robe identifies me as the officiating minister, a part of the wedding party, but not a groomsman or best man. The robe also lends a certain dignity to the occasion.*)

(*Before I went to the robe, I was often asked to wear the frilled shirts, cuffs, etc. Not that I was above it, but the overall impact suggested a candle bearer for a "pop" piano concert, and I just didn't feel comfortable.*)

(*I also discovered that wearing a robe saves me time on the wedding day. I can go to the office, take off my coat, put on my robe, and I'm ready to go. Sometimes at the couple's request, particularly for small weddings, I wear a dark suit.*)

Conclusion

I guess you have gathered by now that a wedding is a big event in my ministry, and I am sure in yours. Other than the preaching experience, leading a person to Christ, or baptizing new believers, there is no public event I share in as supercharged with expectancy as the wedding ceremony. I get excited every time I walk out, and I still get goose bumps when "The Wedding March" begins, and the bride starts down the aisle.

I have witnessed about everything that could happen, from dropping the rings to members of the wedding party fainting, to brides who began to giggle and couldn't stop, to a bride who, after hearing me pronounce them husband and wife, faced the congregation and audibly breathed out so loudly that everyone heard: "At last!"

They have all been exciting, and I am so happy a part of my call and ministry is sharing the wedding event. My prayer is that this manual will be of help to you who share with me this common calling and privilege. May it be conducive in making the weddings you celebrate a witness for Christ, an event to be cherished in the memories of all concerned until the Bridegroom returns for His bride.

Planning the Wedding Ceremony

Orders of Service

I

To Our Wedding Guests

We are honored at your presence with us tonight and are grateful that you will be able to share in this service of worship with us. We come before God and His people to dedicate our lives together to His service—through our union and through fellowship with those who share our journey in life. Our desire is that Christ shall be honored now and in the years to come.

As we take the vows of highest love, we ask that you stand before God to renew the vows of love which you have made to Him—as husband to wife, wife to husband, parent to child—to love those who by virtue of the very essence of life seek the height and depth and breadth of love.

Your presence enriches these moments for us. May they give added dimensions to life as you go from this place.

Names Here

Prelude to Worship

(Script)

If with All Your Hearts	Mendelssohn
Arioso	Bach
Clair de Lune	Debussy
Carillon	Debois
O Perfect Love	Barnby
Prelude on Brother James' Air	Bain
Jesu, Joy of Man's Desiring	Bach
Joyful, Joyful, We Adore Thee	Beethoven

Service of Praise

Call to Worship   **Psalm 8**

O Lord our Lord, how excellent is thy name in all the earth! who hast set thy glory above the heavens. Out of the mouth of babes and sucklings hast thou ordained strength because of thine enemies, that thou mightest still the enemy and the avenger. When I consider thy heavens, the work of thy fingers, the moon and the stars, which thou hast ordained; What is man, that thou art mindful of him? and the son of man, that thou visitest him? For thou hast made him a little lower than the angels, and hast crowned him with glory and honour. Thou madest him to have dominion over the works of thy hands; thou hast put all things

under his feet: All sheep and oxen, yea, and the
beasts of the field; The fowl of the air, and the fish
of the sea, and whatsoever passeth through the
paths of the seas. O Lord our Lord, how excellent
is thy name in all the earth!

Hymn: Praise to the Lord, the Almighty

Praise to the Lord, the Almighty, the King of
creation!
O my soul, praise him, for he is thy health and
salvation!
All ye who hear, Now to his temple draw
near;
Praise him in glad adoration.

Praise to the Lord, who o'er all things so
wondrously reigneth,
Shelters thee under his wings, yea, so gently
sustaineth!
Hast thou not seen How thy desires e'er have
been
Granted in what he ordaineth?

Praise to the Lord, who doth prosper thy work
and defend thee;
Surely his goodness and mercy here daily
attend thee.
Ponder anew What the Almighty can do,
If with his love he befriend thee.

Praise to the Lord, O let all that is in me
adore him!

All that hath life and breath, come now with
   praises before him.
Let the Amen Sound from his people again.
Gladly for aye we adore him. Amen.

—Joachim Neander

Invocation and Lord's Prayer

Service of Dedication

Processional

> Trumpet Voluntary   Purcell
> Rigaudon   Campra

Words from the Bible

> Genesis 2:18,21-23
> Mark 10:5-9
> John 2:1-11
> Ephesians 5:22-29
> 1 Corinthians 13:1-13
> Vocal Prayer
> Prayer of Assisi   Dungan

Service of Holy Matrimony

The Covenant
The Giving in Marriage
The Vows
The Giving of the Rings

The Pronouncement
The Prayer of Dedication
    Wedding Prayer   Williams
The Lighting of the Candle
Recessional
    With Trumpets and Horns   Handel
    The congregation is invited to the reception
    in the fellowship hall.

The Wedding Party

Ministers .... (*List the participants*)
Maid of Honor ....
Best Man ....
Bridesmaids ....
Groomsmen ....
Organist ....
Soloists ....
Guest Book and Programs ....
Pianist ....
Serving ....

II

Walk in Love
As Christ Loved Us
Ephesians 5:2

Minister
Organist   Soloist

Maid of Honor	Best Man
Bridesmaids	Groomsmen

Whatsoever Ye Do, Do All to the Glory of
God.

1 Corinthians 10:31

Our prayer and our desire has been that this
marriage ceremony would bring honor and glory
to God. We have prayed and asked God's guidance about each part of the wedding. We thank all
of you who have prayed for us and with us. And
now we thank God for His faithfulness in answering those prayers.

We are glad that you could join us on this special day and share in our joy at this union.
(*List names of bride and groom, parents if desired.*)

Organ Preludes - Favorite Hymns

Joyful, Joyful, We Adore Thee	Arr. Hopson
Thy Word Is Like a Garden, Lord	Reynolds
When Morning Gilds the Skies	Barnby
God, Who Touchest Earth with Beauty	Lowden
Jesus, Thou Joy of Loving Hearts	Baker

This Is My Father's World	Sheppard

Solos

God, Give Us Christian Homes	McKinney
Happy the Home When God Is There	Dykes
Savior, Like a Shepherd Lead Us	Bradbury

Processional

O Master, Let Me Walk with Thee	Smith

Chiming of Hour

All Hail the Power of Jesus' Name	Ellor
All Hail the Power of Jesus' Name	Holden

Statement of Marriage
Prayer
Charge—Ephesians 5
Marriage Vows

The Lord's Prayer	Congregation

Ring Ceremony—Pronouncement
Prayer

Prayer Solo: The Bond of Love	Skillings

Presentation of Couple
Recessional

Now Thank We All Our
God   Karg-Elert
Reception following in the church fellowship
hall
Walk in Love
As Christ Loved Us
Eph. 5:2

III

Prelude
  Wedding Song   Stookey
  God, a Woman, and a
  Man   Lilly Green
Lighting of Candles
Chiming of the Hour
Seating of Mothers
  Two Candles....................   Sonny Salsbury
Entrance Groom and Groomsmen
Processional (*Please remain seated until bride passes the pew*)
  Trumpet Voluntary ....   Purcell
  Bridal Chorus.................   Wagner
Invocation
Statement of Marriage ....
Sermonette ....
Giving of the Bride
  I Could Never Promise
  You ....   Don Francisco

The Vows and Exchange of Rings
Kneeling Prayer
    The Lord's Prayer ....   Minister
Pronouncement
Lighting of the Unity Candle
Benediction..........................   Pastor
Presentation
Recessional ....   Hallelujah
                                            Chorus

The reception will start immediately following
the ceremony in the fellowship hall.
The bride and groom will join you shortly thereafter.

(Photograph of bride and groom)
Believing that God has chosen us for himself
and for each other, in order to love
and serve him more effectively as one we,
(*names of couple*),
will vow our lives one to another forever
having been drawn together
in the Lord Jesus Christ
united by the Holy Spirit
and sealed in the will of the Father.
"Behold, what manner of love the Father
hath bestowed upon us"
(1 John 3:1).

To Our Guests

Thank you for sharing this special day with us and for witnessing our vows of love that begin our new life together. That so many of our friends and family, especially those who came such great distances, could be here tonight to help us celebrate our marriage means a great deal.

We pray that Christ shall be honored and glorified not just today but for the rest of our lives. We want Him to be the Head of our home and Lord of all. May He bless and enrich your lives with joy and love as much as He has ours through your love, friendship, and generosity.

Finally, we would like to express our gratitude to our parents for their love and guidance. The wonderful memories they have given us, the wisdom taught through our years, and the patience that only parents possess shall never fully be repaid.

We honor them today by our lives and love.

God bless you all,

(Names of Bride and Groom)

Our Wedding Party

Maid of Honor
Best Man
Bridesmaids

Groomsmen
Flower Girl...
Ring Bearer ....

Ceremony Participants

Pastors ....
Pianist/Organist ....
Soloists ....

Reception Participants

Guest Book...
Reception Servers

IV

"Ye Shall Abide in My Love"
(*John 15:10*)

"Oh, magnify the Lord with me, and let us exalt his name together," (Ps. 34:3).

Organ Prelude ....
Seating of Mothers
   The Wedding Song..........
   Chiming of the Hour
   Entrance of Groom and Groomsmen
   Processional
   All Hail the Power of
   Jesus' Name .... Martin
   Bridal Chorus................. Wagner

Welcome

"Surely the Lord is in this place" (*Ex. 28:16*).

Statement of Marriage

Giving of the Bride

  "My Tribute" ....

  Sermonette ....

  The Vows and Exchange
    of Rings

  "That's the Way"............

  Kneeling Prayer

  Lighting of the Unity Candle

  Woman/Man That I

  Love ....

  Benediction......................

  Presentation

  Recessional .... Hallelujah
                                 Chorus

The reception will start immediately following the ceremony in the Fellowship Hall. The bride and groom will join you shortly thereafter.

Our Wedding Party

Maid of Honor

Best Man

Bridesmaids

Ushers and Groomsmen

Flower Girl
Ring Bearer
Musicians
Greeter and Guest Book Attendant
Honorary Bridesmaids
Reception Servers
Dear friends,

We would like to thank each of you from the bottom of our hearts for your attendance tonight, your kindness, your generosity, and especially for your friendship. As we unite in our quest to know God and to preach Christ to the world, we ask that you would be fervent in prayer for us, that we would remain wholeheartedly committed to these two great tasks for the rest of our lives. We praise God for friends who will pray for us continually, for apart from your loving prayers our ministry would be barren. Thank you!

Also, a word of thanks is in order to several people whose names have not appeared elsewhere in the program. They are: (*list of names*).

V

(*typed in script*)

Beautiful the marriage of Christians, two who are one in hope, one in desire, one in the way of life they follow, one in the religion they practice.

They are both servants of the same Master. Nothing divides them, either in flesh or in spirit.

They are two in one flesh, and where there is one flesh there is also one spirit

They pray together, they worship together; instructing one another, strengthening one another.

Side by side they visit God's church; side by side they face difficulties and persecution, share their consolations.

They have no secrets from one another; they never bring sorrow to each other's hearts.

Unembarrassed they visit the sick and assist the needy. They give alms without anxiety.

Psalms and hymns they sing. Hearing and seeing this, Christ rejoices. To such as these He gives His peace.

Where there are two together, there also He is present; and where He is, there evil is not.

—Tertullian
Third Century AD

* * *

The Lighting of the Candles

The Prelude

Organist ....

Pianist ....

Soloist ....

Choir.............................. Sanctuary Choir,
First Baptist Church

The Invocation ....

Responsive Reading No. 617
Prayer
The Processional
Jesu, Joy of Man's Desiring
The Bridal Chorus
The Marriage Covenant
The Giving in Marriage.. Minister
Congregational Hymn .... Love Divine, All
Loves Excelling

> Love divine, all loves excelling,
> Joy of heav'n, to earth come down;
> Fix in us thy humble dwelling;
> All thy faithful mercies crown.

> Jesus, thou art all compassion,
> Pure, unbounded love thou art;
> Visit us, with thy salvation;
> Enter ev'ry trembling heart.

> Finish, then, thy new creation;
> Pure and spotless let us be;
> Let us see thy great salvation
> Perfectly restored in thee:

> Changed from glory into glory,
> Till in heav'n we take our place,
> Till we cast our crowns before thee,
> Lost in wonder, love, and praise.

The Charge to the Bride and Groom
The Vows
The Exchange of Rings

The Prayer of Dedication
The Pronunciation ....
The Recessional
"We Shall Go Out with Joy"

> (*in script:*)
> The parents of the bride request the honor
> of your presence at the reception immediately
> following the ceremony in the fellowship hall
> of the Christian Life Center.

The Wedding Party

Ministers
Maid of Honor
Bridesmaids
Flower Girl
Best Man
Groomsmen
Ushers
Ring Bearer

The gown worn this evening by the bride was
also worn by the bride's mother on her wedding
day, and the gold wedding band given by the
groom was worn by his maternal grandmother.
(*in script*)

The parents of the bride and groom join with
them in expressing their joy for your presence this

evening to celebrate their covenant of Christian marriage.

The Wedding Coordinator

You may want to consider having a wedding coordinator at your church. The person who is chosen for this responsibility should be a member of your church and have the interest and time to devote to the various aspects of the position. In some instances she/he may be a paid worker. Most importantly, she should view weddings as a definite ministry of the church and consider them even as a possible outreach ministry.

Many times the families and some of the friends of the bride and groom may be unchurched, and it is most vital that they see and feel Christian love in their association with your church. There may be occasions when this contact will be the only one some members of the wedding party will have with any church.

The wedding coordinator helps to assure that all will run as smoothly as possible between the church and families and guests involved. By conducting the rehearsal she relieves the pastor of this responsibility. During the time of the wedding she helps to solve any problems that may arise and reassures nervous parents that all is going to be all right. She may also have to help nervous brides and grooms overcome any last-minute jitters.

When the couple has been interviewed by the minister who is to conduct the wedding ceremony and he agrees to perform it, his secretary places the time and location of the ceremony on the church calendar. You may have both a worship center and a chapel. Therefore, you will want to be certain that the proper location of the ceremony, rehearsal, and reception are correctly noted.

At this time each couple is presented with a packet of materials we call "The Wedding Packet." This packet contains a booklet giving pertinent information on church policy regarding weddings, fees, and the like. There is a wedding information form which is to be filled out and returned to the wedding coordinator. You may put any information in this packet you feel will be helpful to the families and the church. At this point the bride is advised to contact the church wedding coordinator as soon as possible and is furnished her name and telephone number.

When contacted, the wedding coordinator may answer many questions by telephone and then set up a later time to go over all the details of the wedding. Quite often the bride is accompanied by her mother or sometimes by the groom.

At this meeting the first priority is to see that

the wedding application form is completed properly, and the correct information has been placed on the church calendar.

It is helpful to acquire a portfolio of as many pictures as possible of your church and of weddings that have been conducted in your church. This helps each bride to see the different ways your church can be decorated and also the various arrangements her attendants can be placed about the altar. Most photographers are happy to furnish you with one eight-by-ten-color picture of a wedding they have photographed at your church at a nominal charge or often at no charge at all.

During this first meeting your wedding coordinator can show the bride these pictures and discuss all of the options available to her. In the event that your church furnishes candelabra, this is the time to decide which ones will be used and how they will be placed in the church. We find it helpful to turn the wedding application form over and record all information on the back. Thus you have everything you need on one sheet of paper. Most brides will appreciate any information on a specific florist, photographer, organist, soloist, or caterer. It is helpful to accumulate a file on people you know to be responsible, who are anxious to cooperate with the church staff in helping to assure the wedding goes as smoothly and pleasantly as possible.

After making sure the wedding application form has been completed correctly and after answering questions from the bride, you will want to discuss the rehearsal and wedding ceremony. Since it is the duty of the wedding coordinator to conduct the rehearsal, you will need to determine exactly how the ceremony is to be conducted and how the bride wants it done. In reference to the actual ceremony, you must check with the minister conducting the wedding to make sure you have a complete understanding of his procedure. In assisting the bride and groom to plan their wedding service, you will want to help them create an atmosphere that will be worshipful and God-glorifying.

It will help when you conduct the rehearsal to have a typed order of service available for reference. Some of the information you will need in order to prepare this sheet is as follows:

1. The names of all the bride's attendants.
2. The names of all the groom's attendants.
3. Who will light the candles and at what time?
4. Who will seat the various members of the wedding party such as bride's parents, groom's parents, and grandparents of both bride and groom?

5. <u>How many pews do we reserve for family?</u>
   <u>(In the event of a large number of reserved</u>
   <u>seats, pew cards are helpful.</u> These can be
   small white cards on which the bride or her
   mother writes the name of the guest and the
   number of the pew on which the guest is to
   be seated. The guest then hands the card to
   the usher on arriving at the church and the
   usher knows immediately where to seat everyone. If your church pews are not num-
   bered, the wedding coordinator can tape a
   small card with the pew number on it to a
   part of the pew that is easily visible to the
   usher as he seats guests.)

6. How many songs will there be and where in
   the service are they to be performed?

7. Is there anyone in the wedding party who
   has a physical problem which will require
   special consideration as to seating or participation?

8. If the flower girl and ring bearer are very
   young, you must decide whether or not to
   allow them to stand through the ceremony.
   If they are to be seated, determine when and
   where.

9. Designate which attendants will be honor
   attendants.

10. Determine how each attendant will enter the
    church, where they will stand during the

ceremony, and how they will form up for the
recessional.

11. If your church does not have a center aisle
     you will need to determine which of the
     aisles you will use for the processional and
     which aisle will be used for the recessional.

12. Will the kneeling bench be used? If so, how
     will it be placed?

13. Will aisle runner be used? If so, which of the
     ushers will be responsible for pulling it? De-
     termine the time that the aisle runner will be
     pulled.

14. Will the unity candle ceremony be used? If
     so, where in the service is the best place for
     it?

15. Will you have printed programs? If so, who
     will be responsible for handing them out to
     the guests?

16. Are there any special family relationships
     that it might be helpful for the wedding
     coordinator to be aware of?

17. Discuss the reception briefly, and remind
     the bride to contact the person at your
     church that is responsible for wedding
     receptions.

In summary, try to secure all of the information
about the wedding that will help you to be supportive as possible to the bride. There will be times
when you will conduct small weddings, and all of

the above will not apply. However, most of the information requested prove beneficial.

Prior to the church rehearsal, the wedding coordinator should give the necessary instructions for the wedding arrangements to the custodial staff so the staff will be aware of their responsibilities for the rehearsal and for the wedding day. If the wedding is to be taped, the necessary information is given to the person who handles sound for the church. It is also the duty of the wedding coordinator to be sure that the bride understands all wedding fees, and that these fees are paid one week before the wedding.

A copy of the procedure sheet should be prepared for each member of the wedding party—the organist, soloist, minister, sound man, and photographer. Thus you are assured that all are aware of the exact procedures. Remind the bride at your meeting that it is essential for all members of the wedding party to be on time for the rehearsal.

On the night of the rehearsal, after you have gathered all members of the wedding party in front of the church, you should welcome them on behalf of your pastor and your church, especially those guests who are from out of town. Always begin your rehearsal time with prayer.

You will want to remind the groomsmen to pick up and try on their tuxedos to make sure they fit, and that all parts of the outfit are together. This will save much confusion if there is a problem, because it can be corrected before the actual day or time of the wedding. Go over details of the seating plan with them, and be sure they understand who they will be seating and where.

If you have groomsmen who have not served as ushers before, it will be helpful to give them an information sheet which spells out what their duties are, giving instructions to help them carry out their responsibilities. Remind them again of the time they are to arrive at the church, where they are to dress if they are dressing at the church, and the time you expect them to meet you in order to begin their duties.

If your bridesmaids are to dress at the church, assign them the room they are expected to use. Remind them to bring everything to the church they will need to wear during the ceremony.

Finally, remind all to be on time for the wedding. You cannot emphasize this too much. Remind them also that once they have arrived at the church you do not want them to leave. If they discover they have forgotten something, they should seek you out and you can see about securing the forgotten article.

Now you are ready to pass out your procedure sheets and review them with the wedding party.

After this review is completed, have each member of the wedding party take their assigned places. After the bride is sure of the order in which every person is to stand, it will be helpful to mark each person's place with a small piece of tape or anything that will stick to your carpet, yet be easy to pull up after the wedding. These markers should stay in place during the wedding. The attendants will feel more confident, especially in a large wedding, if they know they will have the marker to stand on when they reach the altar area.

With all of the attendants in place, you are now ready to start the bride down the aisle on her father's arm. Continue the rehearsal through to the recessional, then begin with the processional. Complete the entire ceremony from beginning to end. By this time, everyone should be comfortable with his/her part on the wedding day. End the rehearsal with another reminder to be punctual the next day.

The Wedding Day

You should arrive one hour before the wedding service. Upon arrival, check the church to make sure all of your instructions have been carried out correctly. The candles, kneeling bench, table for the bride's book, etc., should all be in place. Visit with the bride and make sure she and her attendants have all they need and that all is well with them. Check with the ushers for any last-minute instructions and see that their attire is correct. Be sure their flowers are pinned on properly.

Remain in the foyer or narthex of the church to insure all plans are proceeding on schedule. Give any last-minute instructions to the photographer, seeing that he understands the policy of your church regarding wedding pictures. If any changes have been made in the ceremony during the rehearsal, inform the minister of them. It is a good idea to consult with him when he arrives at the church to go over final details.

If the time of the wedding is only minutes away and you have a large number of guests yet to be seated, it will be wise to close the guest book and immediately usher the guests into the worship center. When you have cleared the area, it will be time for the bride and her attendants to be brought to the area where they will be entering for the service. Always make every effort to begin a wedding on time.

You may want to consult your procedure sheet to be sure of the order in which the attendants are to enter the church. Line them up accordingly and you will be ready to start just after the minister, groom, and best man take their places at the altar.

Send each attendant in according to your plan, and at the proper moment the bride and her father enter. Close the doors to the worship center at this time.

After the service, help the wedding party set up for the pictures. Remain at the front of the church so you may help the photographer if he should need you. Your minister may have delegated the responsibility of securing the proper signatures on the license to you. If so, and you have not already done so, now is a good time to have the honor attendants sign the license. If a copier is available, you may want to make a copy of the license and present it to the bride and groom. An extra copy can be made to keep at the church in the event that the original becomes lost in the mail. After the pictures are taken, help the bride and groom to make their way to the reception.

You will need to decide whether to stay through the reception and assist the happy couple on their way at the end of the reception.

Instructions for Ushers*

The Head Usher is responsible for seeing that ushers arrive at the church on time for the wedding. He makes certain that the best man, groom, and ushers are wearing their boutonnieres. If coats are to be buttoned for the wedding, he makes sure that everyone has his coat buttoned. In general, he checks the ushers' attire and ascertains that all are properly outfitted. He obtains from the bride's mother any special instructions for the seating of the guests in the reserved section. He informs the ushers of the seating plan. He watches the seating at the church to see that guests are seated uniform-ly.

If ushers have not been selected by the bride and groom to perform the special duties, the head usher appoints them at the rehearsal. (*Printed instructions to be given to each usher.*)

1. Light the candles
2. Seat the groom's mother and father
3. Seat the bride's mother
4. Draw aisle ribbon (if used)
5. Pull aisle runner (if used)
6. Return for bride's parents
7. Return for groom's parents
8. Return for honored guests
9. Untie aisle ribbons (if used)

Ushers are to assist the head usher to assure that everything runs smoothly. All ushers should arrive at the church one hour before service starts. *This is very important. Please make every effort to be on time.* Ushers line up at the left of the doors (*as you face the altar*) in the narthex of the church. <u>This will enable you to offer the right arm to lady guests as they approach the doors.</u> The east side of the church is considered to be the bride's side, and the west side of the church is considered to be the groom's section.

We always seat in the center section at First Baptist until guests are seated approximately three fourths of the way back, then we begin to use the side sections. Never seat guests closer to the altar than honored guests are seated. Make certain that you understand who is to be seated in the reserved section or family section. If in doubt, it is better to inquire than to seat family in the incorrect place.

Ushers should talk to guests in a low voice as they escort them to their seats. Be attentive if they request a certain pew. *We do not inquire if they prefer the bride's side or the groom's side.* The exception to this, of course, is when we seat family members.

An usher offers his right arm to the lady guest, seating her in a special section if she is an honored guest or a relative. Guests may express a preference for a certain pew and we try to honor that request as long as it is not in the reserved section. If several guests or couples arrive together and there is a shortage of ushers at the time, an usher offers his right arm to the eldest lady and the other couples will follow, ladies walking in first. He then seats the couples together. Do not proceed back down the aisle until all are seated.

Ladies who arrive together without a male escort are seated individually at the time of their arrival, unless there is a shortage of ushers; in which case, he offers his arm to the eldest lady in the party. Small children are not escorted by an usher; the usher escorts the mother, the child following a few steps behind. Men arriving alone are escorted to their seats. The usher does not offer his arm unless the man is very aged and feeble.

Please do not chew gum at any time during the ceremony. We request that you refrain from arriving at the church under the influence of any alcoholic beverage. We like to be very aware that we are in church and that the atmosphere is somewhat subdued in keeping with the occasion. When in your places at the front of the church, it will help you to stand properly if you place your bodies on an angle and in line with a definite point opposit_____ be _____ processional. When the bride arrives at the altar, you should be watching her. Hands are held crossed, right over left, unless instructions are given to the contrary.

When the bride, groom, best man, maid of honor, and the pastor ascend to the upper level, you turn to face in their direction. You can turn as they begin to walk up to the altar. This way, we can limit all movement to that particular time. *Please remember not to "lock your knees."* When you stiffen your legs too much, circulation is hampered and might cause you to faint. When the ceremony is over and the bride and groom ascend the steps, you turn again to follow their progress. Remember to offer your arm to your bridesmaid as you recess. We recess down the west aisle, across the narthex, to the far east side to await your cue to reenter the church for pictures.

Ushers who are to return for parents or honored guests should release the arm of their escort and wait with the wedding coordinator for your cue to escort your guest. If the guests in the church are not seated all the way to the rear of the church, you may stop about three pews back of the last seated guests and cross over to the proper aisle between the pews. This helps to keep the recessional moving at a good pace, particularly if there are several guests who must be escorted out. The proper order for the recessional is: bride's parents, groom's parents, bride's grandparents, groom's grandparent's, plus any honored guests who are to have a special escort.

Thank you for your cooperation!

Actual Wedding Ceremonies

1

We are gathered today to celebrate one of the happiest moments in the lives of _____(*man*) and _____(*woman*); for on this day, _____ (*man*) and _____(*woman*) affirm before witnesses of earth and heaven that they believe God has purposed that they should share life in the holy bonds of Christian marriage. _____(*man*) and _____(*woman*) desire that God would be honored in their marriage.

Would you join me with them in prayer as we seek God's full blessing upon their relationship?

Prayer

Who gives this woman to be married to this man?

It was in the quiet bowers of the Garden of Eden that God made man in His own image. But the Bible tells us that God saw that it was not good for man to be alone. So with loving care He

removed a bone from Adam's side from which to
fashion Eve. And God brought Eve to Adam.
Thus, the Scripture suggests that God specifically
made Eve for Adam, and Adam for Eve.
_____(*man*) and _____(*woman*), you have
both affirmed that you believe God specifically
purposed you to share life together. As an ac-
knowledgment that you do receive one another as
God's gift, please join hands together.

_____(*man*), it is important for a husband to
learn something about receiving his wife by observing the manner in which God created Eve.
God did not use a bone from Adam's foot to suggest he should "lord it over" the wife. Nor did He
take a bone from his head to suggest that Eve
should "lord it over" the husband. In choosing to
use Adam's rib it is suggested that Eve was created
to share life at Adam's side, close to his heart.
Also, since Adam was created first, it is suggested
that God intends man to initiate spiritual leadership in the home.

_____(*man*), it is your commitment to receive
_____(*woman*) to your side to love her and care
for her, to open your heart and life to her, and to
be the spiritual leader in the home? Do you promise?

"I do."

_____(*woman*), the wife learns something important about her role in marriage and how to receive her husband by also observing the order of creation. Inasmuch as God chose to first create man, then from man made a woman and brought her to man, it is suggested that God's intention is for a wife to truly consider herself as a gift to her husband. This in turn suggests she must trust her husband as leader in the home as the New Testament teaching bears out. Of course, this means that a wife must be submissive to her husband's spiritual authority and leadership in the home.

_____(*woman*), is it your commitment to receive _____(*man*) as your spiritual head and be submissive to his leadership as his supportive and loving wife? Do you promise?

"I do."

As an expression of your commitment today, _____(*man*) and _____(*woman*), you will now exchange wedding rings and vows.

Much is suggested about the quality of your love as we look at the rings. Made of gold, one of the purest of metals, the ring suggests your commitment to unfailing purity and fidelity in your love. So as you wear it, may you be continually reminded of this commitment.

Also, we note that the ring is a complete circle with no separation point. This suggests a commitment on your part to always remain together, to never reject one another. It further suggests an openness to seek to see life from one another's viewpoint with the understanding that each of you makes a vital contribution to the strength and character of the other.

_____(*man*), as you now take the ring from the pages of the Bible (*extend open Bible for bride-groom to take the ring*) to place it on your bride's finger, please repeat these words after me:

_____(*woman*), with this ring I commit all my love to you. As I love the Lord, so do I love you. I receive you as God's gift to me. I receive every quality of your life as purposed by God to perfect virtue in me. As God enables me, I will lead our home spiritually under the lordship of Jesus Christ. I will seek to support and encourage you through each life challenge. All that is mine is yours until death should part us.

Now, _____(*woman*), as you take the ring for _____(*man*) from the Bible to place it on his finger, please repeat these words after me:

_____(*man*), with this ring I commit all my love to you. As I love the Lord, so do I love you. I receive you as God's gift to me. I receive every quality of your life as purposed by God to perfect virtue in me. I trust the Lord to enable me to be submissive to you as my spiritual head and leader of our home. I will seek to support and encourage you through each life challenge. All that is mine is yours until death should part us.

Bride and groom kneel for closing prayer.

2

Minister: Dearly Beloved: We are gathered together here in the sight of God, and in the face of this company, to join together this man and this woman in holy matrimony, which is commended of the apostle Paul to be honorable among all men; and therefore is not by any to be entered into unadvisedly or lightly; but reverently, discreetly, advisedly, and in the fear of God. Into this holy estate, these two persons come now to be joined. (*The following statement is optional.*) If any man can show just cause why they may not lawfully be joined together, let him now speak, or else hereafter forever hold his peace.

(*Now, addressing the persons who are to be married, you say:*)

I require and charge you both, as ye will answer in the great Day of Judgment, when the secrets of all hearts shall be disclosed, that if either of you knows any impediment why ye may not be lawfully joined together in matrimony, ye do now confess it. For be ye well assured, that if any persons are joined together otherwise than as God's Word doth allow, their marriage is not lawful.

(*Pause*) The minister now addresses the groom:

_____(*man*), wilt thou have this woman to be thy wedded wife, to live together after God's ordinance in the holy estate of matrimony? Wilt thou love her, comfort her, honor and keep her, in sickness and in health; and forsaking all others, keep thee only unto her, so long as ye both shall live? (*The man shall answer, "I do," or "I will." Then the minister addresses the woman:*)

_____(*woman*), wilt thou have this man to be thy wedded husband, to live together after God's ordinance in the holy estate of matrimony? Wilt thou obey him, and serve him, love, honor, and keep him in sickness and in health; and forsaking all others, keep thee only unto him, so long as ye both shall live?

(*The woman shall answer, "I do," or "I will." Then the minister shall say:*)

Who giveth this woman to be married to this man? (*The father or person giving the bride can answer "I do," or "I will," or "We do," or "Her mother and I do."*)

(*Then the couple shall exchange their vows in this manner: The minister, receiving the woman at her father's or friend's hand, shall cause the man with his right hand to take the woman by her right hand and to repeat after him as follows:*)

I, _____(*man*), take thee, _____(*woman*), to

my wedded wife; to have and to hold from this day forward, for better, for worse, for richer, for poorer, in sickness and in health, to love and to cherish, till death do us part according to God's holy ordinance; and thereto I plight thee my troth.

(*Then they shall loose their hands, and the minister will ask the woman to take the right hand of the man with her right hand as a symbol of her commitment. She will repeat after the minister:*)

I, _____(*woman*), take thee, _____(*man*), to my wedded husband, to have and to hold from this day forward; for better, for worse, for richer, for poorer, in sickness and in health, to love, to cherish and to obey, till death do us part, according to God's holy ordinance; and thereto I plight thee my troth.

Ring Service:

(*Then they shall again loose their hands. The minister shall take the ring from the best man and place it in the man's hand. The man will then place it on the third finger of the woman's left hand. And the man holding the ring there, shall repeat the following vow as the minister leads:*)

With this ring I thee wed, and with all my worldly goods I thee endow: in the Name of the Father, and of the Son, and of the Holy Ghost. Amen.

(*The minister receives the man's ring from the maid or matron of honor and gives it to the woman. The woman places the ring upon the third finger of the man's left hand. Holding the ring there, she repeats the following vow as the minister leads:*)

With this ring I thee wed, and with all my worldly goods I thee endow: in the Name of the Father, and of the Son, and of the Holy Ghost. Amen.

(*Then the minister shall say:*)

Let us pray:

Our Father, who art in heaven, hallowed be Thy name; Thy kingdom come; Thy will be done on earth as it is in heaven; Give us this day our daily bread, and forgive us our trespasses as we forgive them that trespass against us; and lead us not into temptation; but deliver us from evil. O Eternal God, Creator and Preserver of all mankind, Giver of all spiritual grace, the Author of everlasting life; send Thy blessing upon these Thy servants, this man and woman, whom we bless in Thy name; that as Isaac and Rebecca lived faithfully together, so these persons may surely perform and keep the vow and covenant betwixt them made, whereof this ring given and received is a token and pledge and may ever remain in perfect love and peace together, and live according to thy laws, through Jesus Christ our Lord. Amen.

Then the minister shall join their right hands together and say:

"What therefore God hath joined together, let not man put asunder."

Then the minister shall address the assembled company:

Forasmuch as _____(*man*) and _____(*woman*) have consented together in holy wedlock, and have witnessed the same before God and this company, and hereto have given and pledged their troth, each to the other, and have declared the same by giving and receiving a ring, and by joining hands: I pronounce that they are husband and wife, in the Name of the Father, and of the Son, and of the Holy Ghost. Amen.

(*Optional: The minister can add this blessing, the couple kneeling, and the minister putting his hands upon their heads:*)

God the Father, God the Son, God the Holy Spirit, bless, preserve, and keep you: The Lord mercifully with His favor look upon you, and fill you with all spiritual benediction and grace; that you may so live together in this life, and through faith in our Lord Jesus Christ, life everlasting. Amen.

(*Optional: The unity candle service. As the couple moves toward the unity candles, the minister may say: "Prior to the service, the parents lighted the candles which represent the contributions of love and life itself which they have made in the shaping of their children's lives. From the uniqueness of these separate flames, they kindle a larger, brighter flame which represents the bride and groom's union in Christ. The side candles remain burning to symbolize the continuing importance of family ties and the individual integrity within the marriage relationship. The greater height of the center candle depicts their belief that together in Christ, they can become more than either could alone."*)

(*There are many other options for using the unity candles. This is only one way. It can be very meaningful, particularly if described as above or in similar fashion.*)

3

We have gathered together to celebrate a commitment of love, a commitment that _____ (*man's name*) and _____(*woman's name*) believe to be the leadership of the Holy Spirit in their lives. Let us ask our Heavenly Father to bless this special occasion.

Prayer: Dear Lord: We come into your presence

with thanksgiving and praise. We bless You for the assurance of Your guidance in our lives. We praise You for the awareness that You care about every endeavor of our lives, especially our relationships that lead to Christian marriage. Bless then, this special occasion as _____(*man's name*) and _____(*woman's name*) come before You, their family, and friends to link their lives together in this ceremony of commitment. In Jesus' name, we pray. Amen.

Minister:

A Christian wedding ceremony finds a great deal of instruction, encouragement, guidance, and admonition in the Holy Scriptures.

In the story of Adam and Eve, the second chapter of Genesis adds vital insights to the concept of marriage. This chapter tells how the Lord God formed man from the dust of the earth and breathed into his nostrils the breath of life so that he became a living soul. Then the Lord God placed him in the beautiful Garden of Eden. Something, however, was lacking. The man was not complete in the garden. Then the Lord God said, "It is not good that the man should be alone; I will make him an help meet for him" (*Gen. 2:18*).

This early Bible account points to one of woman's important roles—that of helpmeet to her husband. Wives have rendered valuable help to their husbands in every field of human activity and in every period of the world's history, from the time of Eve to the present. But woman was not created solely to be man's subordinate helper.

After the Lord God had decided to make woman, He caused a deep sleep to fall upon the man. God took one of Adam's ribs, not a part of his head or foot to be ruler or to trample upon her, but from near his heart, of the same substance as man, a coequal, not inferior or superior, but a sharer of life.

In a marriage ceremony with God Himself as the officiating minister, "The Lord God . . . brought her unto the man" (*Gen. 2:22*).

United with woman, man was now complete and whole. No longer were they two people, but one. Adam expressed the closeness of their union when he declared: "This is now bone of my bones, and flesh of my flesh: she shall be called Woman" (*Gen. 2:23*).

Jesus underscored the uniqueness of this first marriage and its continuing importance when He made this penetrating and comprehensive statement: "But from the beginning of creation God made them male and female. For this cause shall a man leave his father and mother, and cleave to his wife; And they twain shall be one flesh, so then they are no more twain, but one flesh. What therefore God hath joined together, let no man put asunder" (*Mark 10:6-9*). God's pattern is clear. One man for one woman till death do them part.

Believing that this couple understands that kind of lifetime love and commitment as taught in God's Word, it is my privilege to ask: "Who gives this woman to be married to this man?"

(*The father or friend giving the bride can answer, "I do," "We do," or "Her mother and I do."*)

Minister: Addressing the man:

_____(*man's name*), do you accept _____ (*woman's name*) as equal to you as a person? Do you find in her the qualities you respect, admire, and share that you believe you can live with for a lifetime? Do you intend to give freely to her and receive freely from her? Do you receive _____(*woman's name*) now to be your wife and do you promise to develop this relationship during your marriage?

(*Man answers: "I do," "Yes," or "I will."*)

(*Minister addresses the woman:*)

_____(*woman's name*), do you accept _____(*man's name*) as an equal to you as a person? Do you find in him the qualities you respect, admire, and share that you believe you can live with for a lifetime? Do you intend to give freely to him and receive freely from him? Do you receive _____(*man's name*) now to be your husband and do you promise to develop this relationship during your marriage?

(*Woman answers: "I do," "Yes," or "I will."*)

(*Minister then asks the man to face the woman and take her by both hands and repeat the following vow of commitment:*)

"I accept you, _____(*woman's name*), as a person and to be my wife, with your strengths, and with your weaknesses, to be loyal to you in health or illness, to share what I have and who I am, to love enough to risk being hurt, to trust when I misunderstand, to weep with you in sorrow, to celebrate with you in joy, and to create life with you in reverence."

(*Minister then asks the woman, as they continue to clasp hands, to repeat a similar vow of commitment:*)

"I accept you _____(*man's name*), as a person and to be my husband, with your strengths, and with your weaknesses, to be loyal to you in health or illness, to share what I have and who I am, to love enough to risk being hurt, to trust when I misunderstand, to weep with you in sorrow, to celebrate with you in joy, and to create life with you in reverence."

Ring Ceremony:

(*The minister takes the ring from the best man*

and gives it to the groom who places it on the third finger of the bride's left hand.)

The minister says:

_____(*woman's name*), the ring which _____(*man's name*) places on your finger is like rings fashioned many centuries ago in the form of a circle, made of a precious metal, signifying the quality of your marriage as made for eternity, by the hand of God. This ring has no ending; so does the love _____(*man's name*) has for you.

Pledge: (*Man repeats after minister*)

"This ring I give you in faith and pledge of our constant love and lasting devotion."

(*The minister takes the ring from the maid or matron of honor and gives it to the bride who places it on the third finger of the groom's left hand.*)

(*The minister says:*)

_____(*man's name*), the ring which _____(*woman's name*) places on your finger is a token of her sincere love for you. This ring is gold, (*or silver, platinum, etc.*) a metal most precious, and least likely to tarnish. This symbol of value is an outward and visible sign of an inward and spiritual grace.

Pledge: (*Woman repeats after minister*)

"This ring I give you in faith or pledge of our constant love and lasting devotion."

Prayer: (*Couple may kneel at the wedding bench*

or the altar, or remain standing as the minister prays.)

Dear Father: Giver of life and love, time and eternity. These two people whom You love very much have made public their vows of commitment to You and to one another. Guard and help them keep these sacred and beautiful vows. Grant them a long life to develop their marriage. Guide them with Your wisdom in their daily lives. May their marriage be all You intend it to be. Give them enough difficulty to keep them dependent on one another and leaning on You; enough joy and sunshine to remind them of the sheer thrill of living in Your will.

Thank you, Father, for meeting us here. We ask our prayer in the name of Jesus Christ our Lord, who demonstrated love in its highest dimension on the Cross of Calvary. Amen.

Couple stands and faces the minister; the minister says: _____*(man's name)*, and _____*(woman's name)*, because you have exchanged sacred vows, because you have given rings as symbols of your commitment to Christian marriage, it is my privilege to pronounce that from this day forward, in the sight of God and man, you are now husband and wife. What God hath joined together, let no man put asunder. God bless you.

(The minister then says: _____*(man's name),*
you may kiss your bride and your wife.)

*(The bride then receives her bridal bouquet from
her maid or matron of honor. The couple faces the
congregation, and the minister says:)* I am happy
to introduce you to Mr. and Mrs. _____.
Recessional Begins and Wedding Party Leaves.

4

Minister: We are together at this place and at this
time to celebrate with *(man's name)*_____
and *(woman's name)*_____ the completeness
of their love. The Book of faith, by which we as
believers in Jesus Christ live, tells us that marriage
is an honored event. For the reason of love a man
and a woman shall leave the home of their birth
to share in love and trust a home of their own.
Paul tells us there are many events and different
feelings in life. Three are eternal: faith, hope, and
love. But love, the love that is of God and from
God, is the greatest of them all. Without the love
of God we would be empty people and lack the
power to face life and its problems. Nor would we
have any real hope for tomorrow.

(Prayer:) Dear Father, for the love and commitment one to another that brings *(man's name)*__
_____ and *(woman's name)*_____ to this
sacred event in their lives and in ours. We are

grateful for the church which cares enough about those things that are sacred, those things that are basic, to provide an atmosphere where a man and a woman can in the company of witnesses commit themselves publicly one to another until the parting of death. We recall that before You ordained the church or any human institution, You ordained the home. Knowing the importance You place on Christian marriage and home, we do now ask You to bless this service, these two who commit themselves to You and Your will, and all of us gathered to share their joy. In Jesus' name, Amen.

Love is a word that contains so much impact, we are often hard put to define it. Someone said that love wants to give, and because it does, its prime goal is to make the other person happy. It is a desire to please the partner. It is the passionate and abiding desire on the part of two persons to produce together and yet spontaneously express their individuality in the context of marriage. Love is the soil and climate in which each can flourish, far superior to what either could achieve alone. As good as these definitions are, perhaps none have achieved the beauty and majesty of the apostle Paul's soaring description of God's kind of love found in 1 Corinthians 13:1-7,13 (NASB).

If I speak with the tongues of men and of angels, but do not have love, I have become a noisy gong or a clanging cymbal. And if I have the gift of prophecy, and know all mysteries and all knowledge; and if I have all faith, so as to remove mountains, but do not have love, I am nothing. And if I give all my possessions to feed the poor, and if I deliver my body to be burned, but do not have love, it profits me nothing. Love is patient, love is kind, and is not jealous; love does not brag and is not arrogant, does not act unbecomingly; it does not seek its own, is not provoked, does not take into account a wrong suffered, does not rejoice in unrighteousness, but rejoices with the truth; bears all things, believes all things, hopes all things, endures all things.

....

But now abide faith, hope, love, these three; but the greatest of these is love.

The kind of homes we need most are those where two lives are being drawn together by a holy love greater than their own. If your commitment has these dimensions, love goes on forever.

Believing that the home you wish to establish is founded on that kind of love, the love of God, it is my privilege to ask:

Who gives this woman to be married to this man? (*Response by father, family member or friend: "I do," etc.*)

Minister: Will you please face each other and join hands. (*Man's name*)_____

_____, would you repeat after me: I, (*man's name*)_____, take you, (*woman's name*)_____, to be my wedded wife. To have and to hold from this day. To care for and to encourage in both good times and bad. I promise to live for Christ and with you in the full awareness of trust and love, and with this commitment, I pledge to you my love.

(*Woman's name*)_____, would you repeat after me: I, (*woman's name*),_____ take you, (*man's name*)_____, to be my wedded husband. To have and to hold from this day. To care for and to encourage in both good times and bad. I promise to live for Christ and with you in the full awareness of trust and love, and with this commitment I pledge to you my love.

Ring Service: These rings are symbols of your commitment of love. They are made of gold, expressing the purity which should always be in your marriage. They are formed in circles, expressing the unending dimension of your love and the eternal love of God. Share these rings now in the full awareness of Christ's love in you and through you.

(*Man's name*)_____, would you place

this ring on (*woman's name*)＿＿＿＿＿＿'s third finger and left hand? Would you hold it there and repeat after me:

(*Woman's name*)＿＿＿＿＿＿, I give this ring, as a visible token of my love, and I give it to you as my own life.

(*Woman's name*)＿＿＿＿＿＿, would you place this ring on (*man's name*)＿＿＿＿＿＿'s third finger, left hand? Would you hold it there and repeat after me: (*man's name*)＿＿＿＿＿＿, I give this ring, as a visible token of my love, and I give it to you, as my own life.

Minister: Let us pray: O Lord, thou who art love, (*man's name and woman's name*)＿＿＿＿＿＿ and ＿＿＿＿＿＿ bring their earthly love to thee. Teach them to know thy loving way, that their love may be like thine. As their love grows in your image, grant them the grace, wisdom and compassion to show others thy love. In the name of our Lord and Savior, Jesus Christ, the highest expression of your love for us. Amen.

Having spoken words of testimony and commitment as to your love, one for the other, I, by the authority of this state and by the commission of God and Christ as a minister of the gospel, declare and proclaim that you, (*man's name*)

_____, and you, (*woman's name*)_____, are husband and wife. What God has joined together in this love, let no man ever attempt to break or destroy. For no one hates his own body, but lovingly cares for it just as Christ cares for His body the church of which we are part.

(*Optional—Solo instrumental or vocal as the couple shares in the candle ceremony.*)

The minister then says: God bless you. I present to you Mr. and Mrs._____.

5

Opening Prayer: Minister:

Dear Heavenly Father: You have promised that where two or three are gathered in your name, you would be present. We believe that. May this wedding service be highlighted with a deep sense of your abiding presence, bring honor and glory to your name, and bless this occasion. In the name of Jesus Christ our Lord. Amen.

Biblical View of Marriage:

We are here today in the presence of our Lord and family and friends to witness the joining of _____ (*man's name*) and _____ (*woman's name*) as husband and wife. We need all to remember that just as the true foundation of the

Christian church is Christ, so the true foundation of a Christian home and marriage is Jesus Christ (*see Eph. 5:23-25*).

Let me take time to share some basic Bible truths about marriage:

(*1*) Marriage is of *divine origin.* Marriage is God's idea and not man's. God Himself performed the first marriage ceremony in the Garden of Eden. God saw Adam and said, "It is not good for the man to be alone" (*Gen. 2:18, NASB*) So He created woman and gave her to him to be his companion, his wife.

Someone said, "Woman was made out of the side of Adam. Not out of his feet to be trampled upon, but out of his side to be equal with him, under his arm to be protected, near his heart to be loved."

And not only is marriage, in general, God's idea, but this marriage, after much counsel and prayer we believe to be of divine origin as well.

(*2*) Marriage is more of a *personal commitment* than a civil contract. Civil contracts have escape clauses, but a spiritual commitment never has any excuse to merit dissolution. As you both gave your individual lives to Jesus Christ in faith, so now you come in faith to commit your lives to one another in marriage.

(*3*) Marriage is better understood as a *process* than as a single act. Genesis 2:21 to 24 says (*NASB*):

> So the Lord God caused a deep sleep to fall upon the man, and he slept; then He took one of his ribs, and closed up the flesh at that place.
>
> And the Lord God fashioned into a woman the rib which He had taken from the man, and brought her to the man.
>
> And the man said, "This is now bone of my bones, And flesh of my flesh; She shall be called Woman, Because she was taken out of Man."
>
> For this cause shall a man leave his father and mother, and shall cleave to his wife; and they shall become one flesh.

Marriage is the blending of two unique personalities in all facets of life and in circumstances of life to form a new and wonderful relationship (*See Eccl. 4:9-12*).

Marriage is not a ninety-day wonder but a life-long process. It is one that should ever be becoming and never arriving. It takes a lifetime to build a Christian home.

(*4*) Marriage is meant to be *permanent*. This is strongly taught in many Bible passages. Divorce only comes because of the hardness of human hearts. It is important you remember the seriousness with which the Heavenly Father looks at the permanency of marriage.

(5) Marriage was thought of highly by our Lord Jesus. He spoke of it occasionally. He performed His first miracle at a wedding feast in Cana of Galilee. What He thinks of highly, so should we. John 2:1-2 says:

> And on the third day there was a wedding in Cana of Galilee; and the mother of Jesus was there; and Jesus also was invited, and His disciples, to the wedding (NASB).

(6) Marriage is the *cornerstone* of an orderly society. It is an honorable estate instituted by God and signifying to us the union which exists between Christ and His church. For this reason, marriage is not to be entered into lightly, but reverently and with confidence of God's approval.

Charges

I charge you, _____(*man's and woman's names*) that you remember this covenant is not only a pledge of faith to each other, but also a promise to God to honor the promises you are about to make to Him and to one another.

I charge you, _____(*man's name*), to love _____(*woman's name*), just as Christ loves His church and gave Himself for it.

I charge you, _____(*woman's name*), to

be submissive to _____(*man's name*), even as the church is obedient to the lordship of Christ.

The Leave Taking

"Who is giving this woman to be married to this man?"

The Scripture Reading:

> Be subject to one another in the fear of Christ.
>
> Wives, be subject to your own husbands, as to the Lord.
>
> For the husband is the head of the wife, as Christ also is head of the church, He himself being the Savior of the body.
>
> But as the church is subject to Christ, so also the wives ought to be to their husbands in everything.
>
> Husbands, love your wives, just as Christ also loved the church and gave Himself up for her;
>
> that He might sanctify her, having cleansed her by the washing of water with the word,
>
> that He might present to Himself the church in all her glory, having no spot or wrinkle or any such thing; but that she should be holy and blameless.
>
> So husbands ought also to love their own wives as their own bodies. He who loves his own wife loves himself;

for no one ever hated his own flesh, but nourishes and cherishes it, just as Christ also does the church,

because we are members of His body. For this cause a man shall leave his father and mother, and shall cleave to his wife; and the two shall become one flesh.

This mystery is great; but I am speaking with reference to Christ and the church.

Nevertheless let each individual among you also love his own wife even as himself; and let the wife see to it that she respect her husband (Eph. 5:21-33, NASB).

The Repeating of Vows

(Join hands.)

I, _____*(man's name)*, receive you, _____*(woman's name)*, to be my wedded wife. I accept you as a precious gift from God. I love you with a love only Christ himself could place within my heart. I promise to give myself to you as Christ gave himself to the church. I wish to have and to hold you from this day forward, for better for worse, for richer for poorer, in sickness and in health, to love and to cherish as long as we both shall live, according to God's holy ordinance.

I, _____*(woman's name)*, receive you,

_____(*man's name*), to be my wedded husband. I accept you as God's gift to me. I love you with a love only Christ Himself could place within my heart. I promise to give myself to you as Christ gave Himself to the church. I wish to have and to hold you from this day forward, for better for worse, for richer for poorer, in sickness and in health, to love and to cherish as long as we both shall live, according to God's holy ordinance.

The Ring Service

Minister: May we now have the rings?

The ring, a golden circlet, has no beginning and no end, which sets forth the eternal nature of real love. Rings are exchanged as a token of love and trust. To a Christian, the ring is a symbol and a reminder of the promises made by the married couple to God and to one another, and to the purity of their love.

Will you take this ring, _____(*man's name*) and place it upon _____'s(*woman's name*) finger, and as you do, repeat to her, after me, these words:
Groom: This ring is a token of my love for you. With this ring, I pledge my life and all I have to you, in the name of the Father, the Son, and the Holy Spirit.
Minister: _____(*woman's name*), will you place

_____'s(*man's name*) on his finger, and as you do, repeat to him, after me, these words:

Bride: This ring is a token of my love for you. With this ring, I pledge my life and all I have to you, in the name of the Father, the Son, and the Holy Spirit.

Prayer at Kneeling Bench (*Song*)

The Pronouncement and Kiss (*Song*)

Minister: And now, having pledged your love and loyalty to each other, and having sealed the pledge with the marriage rings, I do, by the authority vested in me as a minister in the church of the living God, and in conformity with the laws of the state, pronounce you husband and wife.

_____(*man's name*) and _____(*woman's name*), you are no longer two independent persons, but you are now one in the eyes of the Lord. What God has joined together, let no man separate.

Kiss

Lighting of the Unity Candle (*Optional*)

The Presentation

I present to you Mr. and Mrs. _____.

Recessional

6

Minister: We come to this house of worship to celebrate together the marriage of (*man's name*) _____, and (*woman's name*) _____. It is fitting and proper that this marriage ceremony be celebrated in this house of God because (*man's and woman's names*)_____ are servants of God. Not only do they acknowledge His claim on them, they also seek His will in their marriage.

Since God Himself sanctified marriage when He brought together the first man and the first woman, and since the Word of God speaks often of the honor and correctness of marriage, and because God promises blessings on those who are faithful to Him and to each other—this then is a high and holy time for these children of God and for all who love them and share their hopes, prayers, and aspirations for a Christ-centered home and marriage.

All who come to the marriage altar desire to have a happy marriage. The nearest place to heaven in this world is a God-centered home. The opposite is also true. The nearest place to hell on earth is a house where hatred, bitterness, and strife are prominent. More scars are put upon a person's character and heart in an unhappy home than in any other place.

Someone said that a home ruled by God's Word is a place where angels may be asked to stay with us, and they would not find themselves out of place! I know that is the kind of home you both desire. You want heaven in your home. There are three ingredients needed in every marriage in order to put heaven in your home.

The first ingredient is a *present,* a gift. Presents are always important to commemorate special occasions. Don't neglect the giving of presents to each other. But don't forget that some presents are nonmaterial. The giving of yourself, your personhood, your time, your words like "I love you," and "I'm sorry." The gift of total commitment. The gift of praying for each other, the gift of unselfishness, the gift of desiring that the other mate becomes all he or she is capable of becoming in Christ. Our Lord taught us this life-style of giving when He said, "It is more blessed to give than to receive" (*Acts 20:35, NASB*).

The second ingredient is *purpose.* Every one needs a purpose. Every couple needs a purpose. Marriage is not two people standing eye to eye but shoulder to shoulder, looking to similar goals. Competition is good in many areas, but it can kill a marriage. By meaningful worship, prayer, and a lot of communication you will discover God's purposes for your life and your home. I enjoin you to obey Jesus who said, "Seek ye first the kingdom of God, . . . and all these things shall be added unto you" (*Matt. 6:33*).

The third ingredient is *power*. The power is a Person. His name is Jesus Christ. The word *home* in one nation means a shrine of the gods. In the Christian life it means the place where Jesus Christ is Lord. There cannot be a successful home if money, prestige, activity, or even people are more important than Jesus Christ. Without Christ as head of your heart and home, your marriage will probably fail. With Christ as the Power in your heart and home, your marriage cannot fail. Jesus promised: "I am with you always, even to the end of the age" (*Matt. 28:20, NASB*).

Heaven in the home: you can have it with the three ingredients of a present, a purpose, and a power.

Believing that (*man's name*)_____ and (*woman's name*)_____ understand this, and believing that they do not take this step lightly, and believing that they accept each other in a spirit of prayer and declare their marriage before God to be an act of worship, it is my privilege to ask: "Who gives this woman to be married to this man?" (*Father, family member or friend responds with "I do," "We do," "Her mother and I," or any brief words of encouragement he would like to speak at the moment of giving away.*)

The couple with hands joined face each other and repeat the following marriage vows:

Man: "I, (*man's name*)_____ take you, (*woman's name*)_____ as my lawful wife, to walk beside me when things are good and when things are bad. I pledge to you my undying love and constant faithfulness. All I have or hope to have, I give to you as my life partner. I pledge you my help, my support, my love, and my prayers. I pledge to remain faithfully yours until death separates us. I ask God's help in keeping this solemn vow."

Woman: "I, (*woman's name*)_____ take you, (*man's name*)_____ as my lawful husband, to walk beside me when things are good and when things are bad. I pledge to you my undying love and constant faithfulness. All I have or hope to have, I give to you as my life partner. I pledge to you my help, my support, my submission, my love, and my prayers. I pledge to remain faithfully yours until death separates us. I ask God's help in keeping this solemn vow.

Ring Service

Minister: You have shared some beautiful and powerful vows. You will now give and exchange rings as symbols of these vows of faith and love. A marriage ring says I love someone special. It is an outward symbol of an inner commitment, just as baptism symbolizes conversion. The Bible says, "God is love" (*1 John 4:8*). That statement was crystalized in a Person. God showed His love for us by sending His only Son into the world, so that we might have life through Him. This is what love is: it is not that we have loved God, but that He loved us and sent His Son to be the means by which our sins are forgiven.

"Dear friends, if this is how God loved us, then we should love one another." (*1 John 4:9-11, GNB*)

Now, (*man's name*)_____ will you give (*woman's name*)_____ her ring? Do you, (*man's name*)_____ give this ring to (*woman's name*) _____ as a symbol? (*Man answers, "I do."*) (*Woman's name*)_____, do you take this ring as a symbol of (*man's name*)_____'s love for you and will you wear it as a symbol of your love for him? (*Woman answers, "I do."*)

(*Man's name*)_____, will you repeat after me this vow? With this ring I thee wed, and with it I give thee my faithfulness and devotion, and I will love you forever, for my love is of Christ, in the name of the Father, the Son, and the Holy Spirit. Amen.

Minister: Now, (*woman's name*)_____ will you give (*man's name*)_____ his ring? Do you (*woman's name*)_____ give this ring to (*man's name*) _____ as a symbol of your love for him?

(*Woman answers, "I do."*)

(*Man's name*)_____, do you receive this ring as a symbol of (*woman's name*)_____'s love for you and will you wear it as a symbol of your love for her?

(*Man answers, "I do."*)

(*Woman's name*)_____, will you repeat after me this vow? With this ring I thee wed, and with it I give thee my faithfulness and devotion, and I will love you forever, for my love is of Christ; in the name of the Father, the Son, and the Holy Spirit. Amen.

Minister: Would you join me in prayer?

Dear Father, we come to you through Jesus Christ our Lord, the supreme manifestation of Your love. We come to praise and thank You for (*man's name*)_____ and (*woman's name*) _____. We rejoice in their salvation and commitment to the lordship of Jesus Christ. We bless you for their public declaration of faith, love and devotion to You and to one another. We are grateful for their families, their friends, and every person who has expressed their love in some way for these two as they have come to this place and time in their lives.

We ask You that the three ingredients of a happy home will never elude their grasp: the present, the purpose, and the power. May their home so exemplify Christ that others will be strengthened and encouraged by the godly light shining through their lives and from their home. Let them always remember Jesus Christ is Lord. For we pray and ask it in the name that's above every name, Jesus Christ, our Lord. Amen.

(*The couple, if kneeling, will rise and face the minister.*)

Minister: (*man's name and woman's name*) _____, today you have made a lifelong commitment to each other. You have unashamedly shared your vows. You have given beautiful rings as a public demonstration of your love. Believing that it is your desire to have a happy home built on the lordship of Jesus Christ, it is my joy as a minister of the gospel of Jesus Christ to pronounce that from this moment on you are now husband and wife. What the Lord has made inseparable, let no man separate. May the Lord bless you always, in all ways.

(*Man's name*)⎯⎯⎯⎯, you may kiss your bride,
your wife. (*bride receives her bouquet, puts her left
arm through the extended right arm of the groom,
they face the congregation, and the minister says:*)
"It is my privilege to introduce Mr. and Mrs.
⎯⎯⎯⎯⎯⎯."

Recessional.

7

(*The service begins with the minister reading
Psalm 95:1-7, NASB.*)
   O come, let us sing for joy to the Lord;
   Let us shout joyfully to the rock of our
      salvation.
   Let us come before His presence with
      thanksgiving;
   Let us shout joyfully to Him with psalms.
   For the Lord is a great God.
   And a great King above all gods,
   In whose hand are the depths of the earth;
   The peaks of the mountains are His also.
   The sea is His, for it was He who made it;
   And His hands formed the dry land.

   Come, let us worship and bow down;
   Let us kneel before the Lord our Maker.
   For He is our God,
   And we are the people of His pasture,
   And the sheep of His hand.

The Processional:

Invocation by the Minister:

Dear Father and Lord: With praise, joy, thanksgiving, and blessing we enter into this time of worship. Praise You for Your goodness. Praise You for Your love. Praise You for Your provision for Your children. Praise You for Christian homes and Christian marriage. Praise You for making this day possible in the life of _____(*man's name*) and _____(*woman's name*). Praise You for leading them to this holy and sacred moment. Now may we recognize Your love and Your presence as vows and lifetime commitments are made. All that we are we yield to You. Our emotions, our thoughts, our hopes, our dreams, are Yours. Bless this ceremony and all who share in it, that Your name might be exalted. In Jesus' name I pray. Amen.

Minister's Charge to the Couple:

_____(*man's name*) and _____(*woman's name*), today you will begin your life together. You will make vows to Christ and one another. You have every intention of living together faithfully for the rest of your married lives. I can assure you that the vows and commitments you make today will be severely tested along the pathway of life. Those challenges can either make or break your marriage. Be confident that with God's assistance not only can your marriage endure, but it can prosper.

In Joshua 1, there is an account of a man who faced an uncertain future. God gave Joshua three assurances to help him. I believe those same assurances will uplift you as you begin your life together.

First, God told Joshua to depend on the *written page* of His Word. In chapter 1, verses 6-8, he was told to practice its commands, meditate on it day and night, and not to let it depart from his mouth. He was told to try it, think about it, talk about it.

A man once said to a dedicated Christian, "I don't understand it. There is a difference between us. What is it?"

The man humbly but honestly replied: "There is only one letter's difference: the letter *L*. You love the world, and I love the Word."

Second, God displayed His *winning power* when He enabled Joshua and the people to cross the Jordan River on dry ground even though it was at flood tide. The third chapter of Joshua records this mighty miracle. God's reason for this exhibition of His power is seen in verse 7 (*NASB*) when He said, "That they may know that just as I have been with Moses, so I will be with you."

God's power is changeless. You will need His

power in the multitude of pressures that will face you. The strains and stresses of the world will drive you to give up, give in, or to live a life reinforced by His power.

Hundreds of years later, Jesus said to His disciples, "You shall receive power" (*Acts 1:8, NASB*). They did. You will too as you allow the indwelling Christ to be dominant in your life and in your home.

Third, God demonstrated His nearness by revealing His *wonderful presence* to Joshua in the fifth chapter. Joshua was engaged in a military campaign when a man with a drawn sword confronted him. That man identified himself as "captain of the host of the Lord" (*v. 14*). Joshua immediately fell down and worshiped the living Lord.

You will find as the years come and go that the Lord Jesus will meet you in your troubles and your joys, laughter, and your heartaches. He will identify Himself as He did to Joshua and to His disciples when He said, "It is I; be not afraid" (*Matt. 14:27*). As you develop your spiritual life together, you will sense His wonderful presence. To paraphrase an old hymn: He will walk with you, He will talk with you, He will tell you you are His own. The wonderful presence of our living Lord Jesus Christ, His winning power, the written pages of His Word are God's candles of hope and strength for you in a dark world. Believing you are committed to His lordship in your lives, it becomes my privilege to ask:

Minister: Who gives this woman to be married to this man?

Father, family member, or friend responds: "I do," "We do," or "Her mother and I do."

(*Couple faces each other with both hands joined, and the man repeats the following vow to the woman.*)

I, _____(*man's name*) take you, _____ (*woman's name*), to be my cherished wife. I promise you, with all my heart, to walk beside you, in days of adversity, and in days of great happiness, to provide an income for material needs, a shoulder to cry on, and a heart that understands. I will rejoice with you, I will weep with you, I will create life with you in reverence. I commit my love to you; I will grow with you in trust, share possessions, communicate openly and honestly with you. I will be the spiritual leader of our home, I will be faithful to you and you alone until Christ calls me home, and I will seek to create a climate where you can find refuge from fear and strength in a troubled world.

(*The woman repeats the following vow*): I, _____(*woman's name*), take you _____(*man's name*), to be my cherished husband; I give to you the love in my heart, the hope in my soul, the faith of my spirit. I look to you as leader in our home. I submit joyfully to your leadership; I promise full cooperation in building a Christian home. I will support you in your aspirations, pray with you in your trials, share your burdens, and labor with you to make our marriage a joy. I will live close to my Lord, so you may trust me at all times. I will laugh with you in the happy times, comfort you in the sad days, and create life with you in reverence. With you, I will honor our Savior and Lord all of our days.

Ring Service

Minister: (*Holding one of the rings up for all in the congregation to see, says:*) The ring is a symbol of the love you have for each other. Its unending circle represents love's eternal quality and the gold speaks of the purity of real love. It will be a ceaseless reminder of this hour and as a seal of the vows you take, you will now give and receive rings.

Do you, _____(*man's name*) give this ring to _____(*woman's name*) as a visible symbol of your vows and love for her?

(*Man responds:*) I do.

(*Minister asks man to repeat after him:*) This ring I give to you as a promise of keeping my vows and loving you, today, tomorrow, and so long as we shall live. In Jesus' name, Amen.

(*Minister receives ring for the groom from maid of honor and gives it to the woman and asks her:*) Do you, _____(*woman's name*), give this ring to _____(*man's name*), as a symbol of your love and vows to him?

(*Woman responds:*) I do.

(*Minister asks woman to repeat after him:*) This ring, I give to you, as a promise of keeping my vows, and loving you, today, tomorrow, and as long as we shall live. In Jesus' name, Amen.

(*At this point there can be a solo, congregational hymn, pastoral prayer or the lighting of the unity candle.*)

Minister: _____(*man and woman's names*), God's Word teaches, "We love, because He first loved us" (*I John 4:19, NASB*). Because you have received Christ Jesus as your Lord and Savior, because you are committed to building a Christian home, because you have pledged your faith in and love to one another, because you have sealed these marital vows by giving and receiving rings, acting in the authority vested in me by the laws of this state and looking to heaven for divine sanction I pronounce you husband and wife in the presence of God and these assembled witnesses.

May the peace of God rule in your hearts and your home.

Minister to groom: _____(*man's name*), you may now kiss your bride and wife.

After this, the minister says: I am delighted to present to you Mr. and Mrs. _____.

8

Minister: Dear friends, we are assembled here in the presence of God to unite _____(*man's name*) and _____(*woman's name*) in marriage.

The Bible teaches that marriage between a husband and wife is a *powerful* force. Solomon said:

> I am my beloved's,
> And his desire is for me.
>
> "Put me like a seal over your heart,
> Like a seal on your arm.
> For love is as strong as death,
> . . . .
> Many waters cannot quench love,
> Nor will rivers overflow it;
> If a man were to give all the
>   riches of his house for love,
> It would be utterly despised
> (Song of Sol.: 7:10; 8:6-7, NASB).

Outside the power of the redeeming grace of Jesus Christ that brings a person from death to

life, from darkness to light, from self to selfless-
ness, from doubt to faith, from uncertainty to assurance, there is nothing more visibly powerful
than the genuine love of a man and woman in
Christ Jesus. That power gives order to a
household, a community, and a nation. Without
it, the whole fabric of society would be chaos.
With it, homes, communities, institutions, and nations have a comprehensive unifying factor that is
its greatest strength.

The Bible teaches that a Christian marriage is
a *picture* of Christ and His relationship to the
church.

> And I saw the holy city, new Jerusalem, com-
> ing down out of heaven from God, made ready as
> a bride adorned for her husband.
> And one of the seven angels . . . came and
> spoke with me, saying, "Come here, I shall show
> you the bride, the wife of the lamb" (Rev. 21:2,
> 9, NASB).

Our Heavenly Father, in seeking to describe
that intimate, heavenly relationship between Himself and His redeemed people, used the earthly
picture of the bride and bridegroom to give us an
idea of our unique position as His beloved. That
is all the more reason that we should guard our
marital ties. To mar this picture of Christ and His

church by unfaithfulness, divorce, or strife within the union would distort the wonderful picture of Christ's abiding and faithful love for His bride, the church.

The Bible teaches that marriage is to be a permanent relationship of one man and one woman freely and totally committed to each other as companions for life. Our Lord declared that "man shall leave his father and mother, and shall cleave to his wife; and they shall become one flesh" (*Gen. 2:24, NASB*).

God's will and ideal for marriage is that it is a lifetime commitment. Jesus' remarks in the Gospels reaffirmed what God had stated early in the course of the human race. Marriage is divinely instituted, sacred, in the purpose of God, and a lifelong union.

Knowing by counsel with you that you understand that marriage is a powerful force of love, a picture of Christ and His church, and a permanent relationship, and you are committed to those eternal principles, it is my privilege to ask:

Who gives the bride to be married?

Bride's father answers: "I do" or "Her mother and I."

The home is built upon love, which virtue is best portrayed in the thirteenth chapter of Paul's First Letter to the Corinthians.

Love is patient and kind; love is not jealous or boastful; it is not arrogant or rude. Love does not insist on its own way; it is not irritable or resentful; it does not rejoice at wrong, but rejoices in the right. Love bears all things, believes all things, hopes all things, endures all things.

Love never ends; . . . So faith, hope, love abide, these three; but the greatest of these is love (1 Cor. 13:4-13, RSV).

Marriage is a companionship which involves mutual commitment and responsibility. You will share alike in the responsibilities and the joys of life. When companions share a sorrow the sorrow is halved, and when they share a joy the joy is doubled.

You are exhorted to dedicate your home to your Lord and Savior, Jesus Christ. Take His Word, the Bible, for your guide. Give loyal devotion to His church thus uniting the mutual strength of these two most important institutions, living your lives as His willing servants and true happiness will be your temporal and eternal reward.

Prayer of Commitment:

Minister: Dear Father, as _____(*man's name*) and _____(*woman's name*) come now to make this very special and once-in-a-lifetime commitment by the promise of these sacred vows, help them never to forget what they are now speaking. Grant them the desire and will to live out these pledges. In the name of Jesus Christ our Lord, Amen.

(*The minister will ask them to join right hands and take the following vows:*)

Minister to Groom: _____(*man's name*), will you take _____(*woman's name*) to be your wife; will you commit yourself to her happiness and her self-fulfillment as a person, and to her usefulness in God's kingdom; and will you promise to love, honor, trust, and serve her in sickness and in health, in adversity and prosperity, and to be true and loyal to her, so long as you both shall live?

Groom: I will.

Minister to Bride: _____(*woman's name*), will you take _____(*man's name*) to be your husband; will you commit yourself to his happiness and his self-fulfillment as a person, and to his usefulness in God's kingdom; and do you promise to love, honor, trust, and serve him in sickness and in health, in adversity and prosperity, and to be true and loyal to him, so long as you both shall live?

Bride: I will.

(*If the wedding ring is to be used, the bride will hand her bouquet to the maid of honor when the ceremony starts. The engagement ring will be left*

*at home or transferred to the right hand prior to the
processional. The minister will receive the ring from
the groomsman and proceed.)*

Minister: The wedding ring is a symbol of marriage in at least two ways; the purity of gold symbolizes the purity of your love for each other, and
the unending circle symbolizes the unending vows
which you are taking, which may be broken honorably in the sight of God only by death. As a
token of your vows, you will give and receive the
rings.

Minister to Groom: _____(*man's name*), you
will give the ring and repeat after me: _____
(*woman's name*), with this ring I pledge my life
and love to you, in the name of the Father, and of
the Son, and of the Holy Spirit.

(*The groom repeats this.*)

Minister to Bride: _____(*woman's name*), you
will give the ring and repeat after me: _____
(*man's name*), with this ring I pledge my life and
love to you, in the name of the Father, and of the
Son, and of the Holy Spirit.

(*The bride repeats this.*)

Minister: Will both of you please repeat after me:

"Entreat me not to leave you or to return from
following you; for where you go I will go, and
where you lodge I will lodge; your people shall be

my people, and your God my God" (Ruth 1:16, RSV).

Minister: Since they have made these commitments before God and these witnesses, by the authority of God and the laws of the state, I declare that _____(*man's name*) and _____(*woman's name*) are husband and wife.

Minister to Couple: _____(*man's name*) and _____(*woman's name*), you are no longer two independent persons but one; "What therefore God has joined together, let no man separate" (*Matt. 19:6, NASB*).
(*Light Candles*)

Now kneel for closing prayer (*and singing of Lord's Prayer if desired.*)

_____(*man's name*), you may kiss your bride. (*Present Mr. and Mrs. _____ The bride will now take her bouquet from the maid of honor, turn toward her husband, and place her left hand through his right arm, then leave down the center.*)

Invitation to Reception.

9

Minister: (*Addressing congregation*) Dear husband and wife-to-be, parents, family, and friends. We have gathered at this appointed time to be a part of one of the most joyful yet holy moments of this couple's life. Marriage is a mystical union, an holy estate which Christ adorned and beautified with His presence in Cana of Galilee.

(*Address and charge to persons being married:*)

_____(*man's name*) and _____(*woman's name*), we share with you some of the excitement, ecstasy, and expectations of this occasion. You may not remember everything I say to you, but let me share briefly this counsel from God's Word. First Peter 3:8-9 gives this wise counsel for making your home a place of happiness and the fulfilling of your dreams and plans. Peter said:

> To sum up, let all be harmonious, sympathetic, brotherly, kindhearted, and humble in spirit;
> not returning evil for evil, or insult for insult, but giving a blessing instead (NASB).

In these brief verses you find five "lets." "Let all be harmonious." That means of one mind and disposition. You will do all within your power to eliminate discord. Be a peacemaker. There will be struggles for territorial rights, but in marriage you really have no rights. They are surrendered in a mutual submission that desires peace more than rights!

"Let all be sympathetic." This sympathy means to stand in the shoes of the other person. It is a willingness to suffer with or rejoice in the happiness of the other. That kind of compassion goes a long way in fortifying a strong relationship.

"Let all be brotherly." This *brotherly* is a word that is also translated as "love." It means that you are to see each other not just as a housewife or a businessman or a sexual partner, but you are to share and enjoy one another's company. Your spouse is not a second-class citizen, but one you delight in being responsive to in all areas of life.

"Let all be kindhearted." This word is also used to describe Christ; yet you are challenged in the setting of your home to be like Jesus! Tenderhearted, sensitive, affectionate. There may be times when you feel the other is deserving of anger and criticism, but the admonition from God's Word is not to retaliate. Instead, be kindhearted.

"Let all be humble in spirit." This is a peculiarly biblical virtue. It is an attribute of Christ and also a spirit which He rewards, for He promised in the Sermon on the Mount that the possessors of this spirit received a unique reward, "Theirs is the kingdom of heaven" (*Matt. 5:3, NASB*).

Peter concludes with two all-important principles. One deals with actions: "not returning evil for evil." The second deals with words: "or insult for insult." Give a blessing instead of an insult or wrong action!

If you practice these principles you'll not only

get along, you will experience all that the Lord wants to grant you in your prayers for a Christ-centered home.

(*Minister then addresses man.*)

You,_____(*man's name*), and you, _____
(*woman's name*), have come to me signifying your desire to be formally united in marriage, and being assured that no legal, moral, or religious barriers hinder this proper union I ask:

Do you, _____(*man's name*), in taking this woman to be your lawful and wedded wife promise to love and cherish her, to honor and sustain her, in sickness and in health, in poverty as in wealth, in the bad that may darken your days, in the good that may lighten your ways, and to be true to her in all things until death alone shall part you? Do you so promise and make this commitment to Christ and to _____(*woman's name*)?

(*Man responds with, "I do."*)

(*Minister then addresses woman:*)

Do you, _____(*woman's name*), in taking this man to be your lawful and wedded husband promise to love and cherish him, to honor and sustain him, in sickness as in health, in poverty as in wealth, in the bad that may darken your days, in the good that may lighten your ways, and to be true to him in all things until death alone shall part you? Do you promise and make this commitment to Christ and to _____(*man's name*)?

(*Woman responds with, "I do."*)

(*Minister addresses the father or whoever gives the woman in marriage:*)

Minister: It is my privilege and obligation to ask: Who giveth this woman to be married to this man?

(*The father or whoever gives her in marriage responds: "I do," "We do," or "Her mother and I do."*)

(*The couple joins right hands and faces the minister. The minister takes the ring from the best man and says:*)

Minister: This ring is very special. You have chosen it with careful attention and consideration. It is and will always be a precious reminder of this holy occasion.

_____(*man's name*), as you receive this ring will you place it on _____(*woman's name*)'s finger and repeat after me to her your vow: (*Man places ring on third finger of left hand and holds it there as he repeats his vow.*)

I, _____(*man's name*), take you, _____ (*woman's name*), to be my wedded wife, to have and to hold from this day forward, in times of plenty, or in times of poverty, in great wealth or in simplicity, in health and sickness, I will love you; I will cherish each meaningful day that God unfolds to us, depending on his provision and grace. I will celebrate the joyous moments with you, and weep with you in sorrow and trouble. I will be faithful to you and to you alone till in death do we part, according to our Father's holy ordinance, and thereto I pledge you my faith.

(*Minister receives ring from maid of honor and says:*) This ring is very special to you. Prayerfully and joyfully you selected it to represent your vows and your love for your husband. It is and always will be a precious reminder of this holy occasion.

_____(*woman's name*), as you receive this ring will you place it on _____(*man's name*)'s finger and repeat after me to him your vow: (*Woman places ring on third finger of left hand and holds it there as she repeats her vow.*)

I, _____(*woman's name*), take you, _____(*man's name*), to be my wedded husband, to have and to hold from this day forward, in times of plenty, or in times when material blessings are few; in great wealth or simplicity, in health and sickness, I will love you; I will cherish each meaningful day that God unfolds to us, depending on His provision and grace. I will celebrate the joyous moments with you, and weep with you in sorrow and trouble. I will be faithful to you and to you alone till in death do we part,

according to our Father's holy ordinance, and
thereto I pledge you my faith.

Prayer:

(*Minister addresses couple, wedding party, and assembled witnesses.*) Forasmuch as _____(*man's
name*) and _____(*woman's name*) have made
mutual vows of faith to Christ and to one another,
and have witnessed the same by the exchanging of
rings as an outward and visible sign of their inward and spiritual pledge, to signify to all the
uniting of their lives in holy matrimony, by the
laws invested in me by the state and as a minister
of the gospel of our Lord Jesus Christ, it is my
privilege to pronounce you husband and wife
together, in the name of the Father, and of the
Son, and of the Holy Spirit. Amen.

(*The couple may choose to kiss at this point, after
which the minister says:*)

I am happy to introduce and present to you Mr.
and Mrs. _____.

10

Prayer: (*Minister*)

Charge to Couple: (*By Minister*)

Beloved friends in Christ: This special moment
has arrived. A moment that a short time ago
seemed like an eternity away is now happening.

Let us do everything we can to taste the joy of this once-in-a-lifetime experience. I want to do that by not only leading you in your vows but also by sharing a challenge with you from the Word of God. Let me begin by asking you a question:

Do you acknowledge the lordship of Christ and that you believe it to be God's will for you to marry?

(*Couple answers aloud together, "We do."*)

Minister: Your marriage is taking place in a society that has lost respect for the vows and for the keeping of the principles that guarantee a happy and enduring marriage. A major magazine had a lead article entitled: "The American Family— Can it Survive Today's Shocks?" Many do not; but yours can. Let me share, as a reminder, some principles that will not only let your marriage survive but allow it to prosper.

The first principle: God must make a marriage. He established it as a divine institution and ordained that Christians should marry Christians. The apostle Paul said, "Do not be bound together with unbelievers" (*2 Cor. 6:14, NASB*). A couple with a personal relationship to Jesus Christ through faith in Him and repentance from sin have the best chance of succeeding in the process of building a lasting marriage.

The second principle: There is to be a mutual

submission. Ephesians 5:21 says, "Be subject to one another in the fear of Christ" (*NASB*). This does not eliminate the principles of the man being the spiritual leader in the home, but it is a careful reminder that the attitude of both partners is to be one of a mutually submissive spirit. That kind of heart keeps a husband from being a dictator and a wife from being the domineering force in the home.

The third principle: God intends in His perfect will that marriage is to be a permanent affair. In Genesis 2:24, the Lord God said that a man should "cleave unto his wife." Ordinarily, we think of a cleavage as a parting, but in biblical terms it means to adhere to—stick together no matter what! The contemporary mentality is if it doesn't work out, bail out. God's counsel is to commit yourselves to permanency.

The fourth principle: Develop your communication. A famous psychologist said that the most frequent fault in marriages seems to be the lack of complete frankness and mutual openness. Genesis 2:25 says that "the man and his wife were both naked and were not ashamed." I believe there are two interpretations of this statement. First, they were not ashamed of their sexuality; second, there is a symbolic understanding. Adam and Eve were open and honest with one another. Before the fall, they had a beautiful frankness and openness. After their sin, they tried to cover up and even blamed each other for their disobedience. Work at and develop your communication. It will be one of your strongest allies in making your marriage strong.

The fifth and final principle: Remember, marriage is a process. Genesis 2:24 reminds us that "they shall become one flesh" (*NASB*). There is nothing magical in repeating a vow. The real developing of your marriage into Christlikeness will take the rest of your lives. The two of you must patiently build the walls of your marriage one day at a time. In that process, you will become one flesh.

(*The minister then asks the parents to stand and asks them the following question:*) By acknowledging that children are a heritage from the Lord, and you have faithfully given of yourselves to bring these, your children, up in the nurture and admonition of the Lord, do you now recognize the leadership of the Holy Spirit in their lives, and do you now enter into their joy, by giving your blessing to their union?"

(*Both parents answer out loud, "We do." The minister can have them repeat it together or look to the bride's parents for the first response, then to the groom's parents.*)

Minister: Who gives this woman to be married to this man?

(*Father, family member, or friend replies: "I do," "We do," or "Her mother and I do.")*

Minister: Will you face each other, join your hands, and repeat after me your vows to the Lord and to one another?

I,_____(*man's name*), offer myself completely to you, _____(*woman's name*), to be your husband in marriage. I promise to love you with all of my heart, and to be true and faithful, patient, kind, and unselfish in this love. I promise to stand beside you always, in times of joy, in times of trial, and in times of sorrow. I dedicate our marriage and our home to the lordship of Jesus Christ. I pledge myself and all that I am in love.

(*Minister turns to the woman and leads her in repeating her vow to the man.*)

I, _____(*woman's name*), offer myself completely to you, _____(*man's name*), to be your wife in marriage. I promise to love you with all of my heart, and to be true and faithful, patient, kind, and unselfish in this love. I promise to stand beside you always, in times of joy, in times of trial, and in times of sorrow. I dedicate our marriage and our home to the lordship of Jesus Christ. I pledge myself and all that I am in love.

Ring Vows: (*Minister takes the ring from the best*

man, hands it to the man who places it on the woman's third finger on her left hand.)

Minister: (*to the man*) Because you desire to symbolize your sacred vows, I ask you to repeat after me and to _____(*woman's name*) your ring vow as you hold this ring on her finger.

This ring I give you in faith and pledge of our constant love and lasting devotion. It is symbolic of my sacred vows to our Lord Jesus Christ and to you. In the name of the Father, the Son, and the Holy Spirit. Amen.

Minister: (*to the woman*) Because you desire to symbolize your sacred vow, I am going to ask you to repeat after me and to _____(*man's name*) your ring vow as you hold this ring on his finger.

This ring I give you in faith and pledge of our constant love and lasting devotion. It is symbolic of my sacred vows to our Lord Jesus Christ and to you. In the name of the Father, the Son, and the Holy Spirit. Amen.

(*Prayer as the couple kneels, or music and prayer. The pastor then asks the couple to rise and face him.*)

Minister: _____(*man's name*) and _____ (*woman's name*), I require and charge you both, as you stand in the presence of God, your family, and these assembled witnesses to keep these solemn vows inviolate and to be steadfast in your endeavors to build a marriage that brings glory to God and joy to your family and all of those who know and love you. Believing that is your deepest intention, it is my privilege as a minister of the gospel and by the authority invested in me by the laws of this state to pronounce from this day forward that you are now husband and wife. We pray for you a blessed marriage.

(The Minister may then invite the man to kiss his wife and bride, then turn them toward the audience and introduce them.)

Minister: I am happy to present and introduce you to Mr. and Mrs. _____.

11

Minister: Welcome to this service of praise and worship. The reason that this gathering is being held today and the reason for which you have come is to give honor and glory to the name of the Lord Jesus. The psalmist wrote:

Praise the Lord! Praise, O servants of the Lord. Praise the name of the Lord. Blessed be the name of the Lord from this time forth and forever. From the rising of the sun to its setting the name of the Lord is to be praised. The Lord is high above all nations; His glory is above the heavens (Ps. 113:1-4, NASB).

The apostle Paul wrote:

> Oh, the depth of the riches of the wisdom and knowledge of God! How unsearchable are his judgments, and his paths beyond tracing out! For from him and through him and to him are all things. To him be glory forever! Amen (Rom. 11:33-36, NIV).

Dear friends, it is this almighty, awesome, and holy God that _____(*man's name*) and _____(*woman's name*) love with all their hearts. It is in the presence of this God that we have met today. Let us join our hearts in prayer:

Prayer: Dear Father: In the Spirit of Christ, and with a profound sense of your presence, may you receive the honor and glory due to you in this wedding ceremony; may each of us magnify the Lord. Let us exalt your name together. In the name that is above every name, Jesus Christ, our Lord, we pray. Amen.

Minister: _____(*man's name*) and _____ (*woman's name*) have come here today to be joined together in marriage. They want their union to be a complete, total union, and it will be complete because both are committed to Jesus Christ as the only Lord of their lives. Believing this to be true, it is my responsibility to ask, Who gives this woman to be married to this man?

(Father, friend or member of family answers: "I do," "We do," or "Her mother and I do.")

Minister's Charge: _____(man's name) and _____(woman's name), you can never be fully married to another person until you are thoroughly married to Christ. Married persons outside of Christ can only give two-thirds of their lives to the other, the body and soul. Without Christ and His indwelling Spirit, they cannot share together their total lives.

The Bible teaches that marriage should exemplify the relationship of Christ with His church, and that relationship is primarily a spiritual one. The union of spirits is the foundation of the marriage, not the icing on the cake.

Other than the spiritual union, there are several other characteristics of Christ's relationship to the church which should be present in all marriages. For those of you who are married, you may want to compare these qualities to your own marriage; and if you see some areas that need improvement, we encourage you to renew your vows to your spouse while _____(man's name) and _____(woman's name) recite theirs in just a few moments.

In Ephesians, chapter 5, we see the picture of Christ's love to the church symbolic of the groom's to the bride. In verse 25 there are two words: "just as" (*NASB*). The husband loves his wife "just as" Christ loved the church. That means God loves us as we are. It is an unconditional love. We come to Christ "just as" we are, "without one plea, But that [His] blood was shed for me." The husband loves his wife unconditionally.

That love is a sacrificial love. Jesus died a grueling death in our place. The Bible says that He "gave Himself up for her" (*v. 25, NASB*). He put us ahead of Himself. Even so must the husband give himself sacrificially to his wife. He sacrifices time, wishes, energies, the very best that he has for his wife.

That Christlike love is also a love that offers itself to better the other person. The apostle Paul said that Christ wants to present us "to Himself the church in all her glory, having no spot or wrinkle or any such thing" (*Eph. 5:27, NASB*). Christ takes us where we are and begins to change us for the better in actions, attitudes, and total life-style. A good husband will disciple his wife, offering every help he can to see his wife develop to the highest spiritual potential she can possibly achieve.

In turn, this powerful passage also presents the church's response to Christ, or the bride to the bridegroom.

The bride is to have a sense of dependence upon the husband. God's Word says that Christ "nourishes and cherishes" the church" (*v. 29*). God demands that we look to Him for every need. That begins at salvation and continues throughout our lifetime.

The bride, then, is to look to the hand of her husband for all her needs and protection. This dependence strengthens the couple in building a fabric of interdependence. The demand for independence has broken many homes. This position does not show weakness but builds up strength.

The bride is to be submissive to the husband's spiritual authority and leadership. "As the church is subject to Christ, so also the wives ought to be to their husbands in everything" (*v. 24, NASB*). Jesus Christ is Lord of the church. All followers must allow Him complete lordship over their lives to reach our fullest potential and receive the greatest blessings. This simple spiritual premise, if followed, brings to a marriage its fullest potential and blessing. If not, it can turn the marriage duet into a duel.

The bride gives possession of herself to the groom. Verse 31 (*NASB*) states: "For this cause a man shall leave his father and mother, and shall cleave to his wife." The Bible says that a Christian is not his own because he has been "bought with a price" (*1 Cor. 6:20*). Christ paid for us with His own blood. The one who pays the price owns the merchandise. Thus, the Groom has given His utmost for our highest.

In the marriage realm, the groom turns his back on all others and gives himself to that one person. The bride in turn responds to that sacrifice by surrendering all she has to the man who has committed his life in totality to that union.

Jesus Christ asks from everyone the type of commitment that _____(*woman's name*) is making to _____(*man's name*). He is asking, "Will you marry me? Will you be loyal to me for the rest of your life? Will you allow me to be Lord of every possession, ambition, and dream in your life?" If you say yes, a meaningful life and all of heaven is open to you.

(*Some couples have asked the minister to give a brief invitation at this point inviting the guests to receive Christ as their Lord and Savior as the minister leads in the sinner's prayer.*)

Minister: Will you join your hands and repeat after me? (*Man responds first.*)

I, _____(*man's name*), promise that as long as the two of us live, I will readily accept my privilege and responsibility as the *spiritual head* of our home. I will be the initiator of spiritual matters in our new family, by leading our devotions, by setting an example of holy, godly living before you and our children, by seeking the Lord diligently concerning our welfare as a family unit, and by striving to keep my personal walk with Christ fresh, intimate, and up-to-date.

I also accept the responsibility of *protecting* you and our family from any threat to their physical, mental, emotional, or spiritual well-being. I will also make it my practice, as *provider* for my home, to order our family's finances in such a way, based upon the Scriptures, that our Lord will provide our every need.

I promise to do my absolute best to order my *priorities* so that the Lord Jesus will be first, you will be second, our children third, and our ministry fourth.

I promise to *love* you, as an act of my will, for the rest of my life in the presence or absence of romantic feelings. I choose you, _____(*woman's name*), over every woman I have ever met or ever will meet to be my wife. As long as I live I will do my best to never raise my voice to you in a negative way, and never to belittle you, but rather to *encourage, edify,* and *inspire* you to heights of holiness in your life-style and depths of commitment to our precious Lord Jesus.

(*Woman's vows:*)

I, _____(*woman's name*), pledge to you,

_____(man's name), myself as your helpmate for life according to God's ordained plan for our lives together. In doing so, I will be your encourager, in times of fruitfulness as well as disappointment. I will strive to inspire you to the heights that our Heavenly Father wills you to be motivated. My hope in you will be the confidence I have in trusting God for our future. Because of the respect I've gained for you, I joyfully pledge to you my submissive spirit which falls under the authority given to you by God's chain of command. In knowing you as a man after God's own heart, I pledge obedience to you in the decisions which we will need to make jointly or individually. I choose to stand behind you to support, and beside you to comfort, as we learn and live, viewing this life from God's perspective. I will always honor you as the head of our household as Christ is Head of the church. I give my body fully, totally, and unselfishly to you to satisfy, fulfill, and love you all the days of our lives.

All my life I promise to love, bear, and raise our children as God chooses; because of all these things, I can pledge all my love to you, knowing it is a complex combination of the above qualities —only perfected by our Lord Jesus who will allow us to experience all this and more by His marvelous grace.

Ring Vows: (*Minister*) As a tangible illustration of the vows you have exchanged, you will now give a ring. (*Minister takes ring from best man and gives it to the man, who places it on the third finger of the woman's hand.*)

Minister: (*To man*) Repeat after me: This ring is an expression of all I have promised you. I give it with all my love and life-long commitment. In the name of the Father, the Son, and the Holy Spirit. Amen.

(*Minister takes ring from maid matron of honor and gives it to the woman who places it on the third finger of the man's left hand.*)

Minister: (*To woman*) Repeat after me: This ring is an expression of all I have promised you. I give it with all my love and lifelong commitment. In the name of the Father, the Son, and the Holy Spirit. Amen.

(*Minister asks couple to kneel and placing his hands on their heads he prays.*)

Prayer:

"The Lord bless you, and keep you; The Lord make His face shine on you, And be gracious to you; The Lord lift up His countenance on you, And give you peace" (Num. 6:24-26, NASB).

(*Couple rises and faces minister.*)

_____(*man's name*) and _____(*woman's*

name) Because your love is built on the guidelines and commitments of the Word of God, because you have made public your commitments to Christ and to each other in building a home to mirror Christ's love for His church, it is my privileged honor to pronounce you husband and wife from this day forward. God bless you as you grow together in His likeness.

(*Minister may then give permission for the husband to kiss his wife and if so desired to introduce and present them to the assembled witnesses as Mr. and Mrs. _____.*)

12

Minister: Would you join me in prayer as we ask God's favor and blessing on this wedding service? Dear Heavenly Father: You have ordained marriage. You confirmed it by your gracious presence and miraculous blessing at the wedding in Cana of Galilee. As these two come now to unite their hearts and lives into a sacred, unbreakable union; as they dedicate their home, their children, and their lives to the loving service of Christ Jesus our Lord, do bless us all as we share together in this glad hour. In Jesus' name, Amen.

(*Minister continues*) Psalm 127 is a great psalm and very pertinent to what is happening at this altar and in the lives of these two people. Solomon said:

> "Unless the Lord builds the house, They labor in vain who build it; Unless the Lord guards the city, The watchman keeps awake in vain. It is vain for you to rise up early, To retire late, To eat the bread of painful labors; For He gives to His beloved even in his sleep. Behold, children are a gift of the Lord; The fruit of the womb is a reward. Like arrows in the hand of a warrior, So are the children of one's youth. How blessed is the man whose quiver is full of them; They shall not be ashamed, When they speak with their enemies in the gate" (Ps. 127, NASB).

The insights of Solomon are very helpful as we gather to celebrate your union. It is your chief desire to have a godly home. Notice that Solomon said if that is to be true, it must have a divine Author: "Except the Lord build the house."

Couples who seek to enter a relationship and ignore this truth entertain a serious risk. God intends for marriage to be founded on a personal commitment to Christ, His church, and His will in the home. Marriage is God's recognition of the necessity for the consummation of human love and the continuation of the human race in a well-ordered fashion. To ignore this fundamental truth is to insure domestic chaos and disorder in any society.

Solomon acknowledges another eternal truth. The home must be divinely protected: "Unless the Lord guards the city." The home you are establishing can only endure in the watchful care of God. That does not mean you have no responsibilities in building and defending your home. You do. There are many adversaries to the biblical pattern for the home. The only thing going for you in today's world is the assurance that God is for you in your desire to have a Christian home. You can assist Him as you dedicate your lives today and as you rededicate your home often in the years ahead. Let me strongly encourage you to make prayer, Bible study, service to Christ's church, and family devotions an integral part of your marriage.

Solomon then encouraged you to be divinely content when he speaks of the vanity of ceaseless labor and long hours. Many homes have been broken on the altar of possessions. Material prosperity is not a sin; but if it demands first allegiance, encroaching on your home and church life, it will soon capture, then destroy your joy. Solomon gave wise counsel. Don't worry about what you don't have. Trust the Lord for what you do not possess. Possess your possessions. Don't let them or the desire for them possess you. Practice Paul's art of contentment—"I have learned to be content in whatever circumstances I am" (*Phil. 4:11, NASB*).

The wise psalmist then closed with a word of a divine endorsement—children! The latter section of the psalm highlights the desirability of children in a home. In an age when children seem to have become a liability rather than an asset, when life has been cheapened by abortion and other symptoms of selfish individual human liberty, notice that heaven considers them a blessing. Someone has said that at one time in our past we had families, now we only have samples!

If God blesses your home with children, don't neglect your parental responsibility. The illustration of children being "arrows in the hand" (*v. 4*) is a reminder that the flight of an arrow depends on the way it is produced, the way it is pointed, and the way it is projected. That is your God-given responsibility. "Train up a child in the way he should go, even when he is old he will not depart from it" (*Prov. 22:6, NASB*). A paraphrase could read: "Prepare, point, polish, and project your arrows (*your children*) toward the right goal, and they won't miss the mark!"

You have declared your intention to give to the Lord a home like the psalmist described. It is my privilege then to ask, Who gives this woman to be married to this man?

(*Father, family member or friend responds with "I do," "We do," or "Her mother and I do."*)

(*The minister asks the couple to join hands, face each other and repeat their vows.*)

(*Man begins:*) (*Woman's name*) _____, I love you as Christ loves us, unconditionally, unselfishly, and eternally. I receive you as my wife, my helpmate, a gift from God. Using God's Word as my guide, I promise to be the head and spiritual leader of our home, to protect, respect, cherish, and provide for you. I commit myself to do these things through the power of the Holy Spirit for all of my life.

(*The woman repeats her vow after the minister.*)

(*Man's name*) _____, I love you as Christ loves us, unconditionally, unselfishly, and eternally. I receive you as my husband. I will submit to you as my head and accept you as my spiritual leader. I promise to honor, respect, exhort, trust, and provide a loving and a happy home for you. I commit myself to do these things through the power of the Holy Spirit for all of my life.

(*Couple loose hands and face minister.*)

The minister receives the ring from the best man and gives it to the man who places it on the third finger of the woman's left hand and repeats after the minister:

(*Woman's name*) _____, in token and pledge of our constant faith and abiding love, as your husband I promise to live out these vows.

(*Minister receives ring from the maid/matron of honor and gives it to the woman who places it on the third finger of the man's left hand and repeats after the minister:*)

(*Man's name*) _____, in token and pledge of our constant faith and abiding love, as your wife I promise to live out these vows.

Minister: Let us pray. Bless, O Lord, the giving of these rings that they who wear them may abide in your peace and continue in your favor, and by your strength and their obedience keep these vows for as long as they shall live. To your everlasting glory I pray in Jesus' name. Amen.

Forasmuch as these two have linked their destinies in this holy contract and have combined their commitments to Christ and one another in the presence of God and their loved ones and friends, and have done so reverently, prayerfully, and in the fear of God, it is my privilege as a minister of the gospel of Jesus Christ to pronounce that in the sight of God and humanity you are now husband and wife.

(*Minister may then give permission for the husband*

*to kiss his wife and if so desired to introduce them
to the assembled witnesses as Mr. and Mrs.*
_____.)

13

Minister: The Bible is full of inspiration, guidance, exhortation, and encouragement about the
family. From Genesis to Revelation we read of our
Heavenly Father's deep interest in the well-being
of the first institution—the family. Hear these
words from Psalm 128:1-6 (*NASB*), words of
promise and blessing concerning the home:

> How blessed is everyone who
>   fears the Lord;
> Who walks in His ways.
> When you shall eat of the
>   fruit of your hands,
> You will be happy and it will
>   be well with you.
> Your wife shall be like a
>   fruitful vine within your
>   house.
> Your children like olive
>   plants around your table.
> Behold, for thus shall the
>   man be blessed who fears
>   the Lord.
> The Lord bless you from Zion,

And may you see the
prosperity of Jerusalem all
the days of your life.
Indeed, may you see your
children's children.
Peace be upon Israel!

Would you join me now in a prayer of invocation?

Dear Father and Lord: Our Maker and Redeemer, we come into Your presence knowing that You are the wellspring of life. You are our dwelling place in all generations. Look with favor upon this service, and may the counsel of the psalmist concerning the fear of the Lord and the blessing that results be a constant reminder to these about to become one in Christ, and upon all of us who share in this meaningful hour. In Jesus' name we pray. Amen.

Minister: (*Charge to the couple.*)

_____(*man's name*) and _____(*woman's name*), God's Word is full of promises. It has been said that there are more than thirty thousand promises in the Bible. For the two of you, I want to share a promise from God that I trust will encourage you as you walk life's pathway together. It is found in Philippians 4:19: "My God shall supply all your need according to his riches in glory by Christ Jesus." That is one of the Bible's greatest promises.

It is a *personal promise:* "my God." It is not any god or a god, but *my* God. Augustine said that the Christian faith was built around personal pronouns! This great God who revealed Himself to humanity in Jesus Christ becomes real to us when we repent of our sins and trust Jesus Christ as Lord and Savior. That experience allows us to become "sons of God." That personal relationship enables us to call Him "my God."

It is also a *positive promise.* God "will supply" all your need. That literally means fill up to the full. God's promise to you is positive. You can count on Him. A poet put it this way:

> His love has no limit,
> His grace has no measure;
> His power no boundary known
>   unto men.
> For out of His infinite riches
>   in Jesus
> He giveth, and giveth, and giveth
>   again.

This is a *providential promise:* "all your need." From the cradle to the grave we are a bundle of needs. As the layers of life are peeled off, each fresh unwrapping brings to light new needs. The need for forgiveness, for closer fellowship with God, for grace in trials, strength in temptations, deliverance from evil—all of these and more you will need. God's promise is that by His sovereignty He will meet every need.

This is also a *plenteous promise:* "according to His riches in glory." The Bible speaks of the richness of Christ's goodness, His wisdom, His grace, His glory. The Lord promises to bring all of the resources of heaven to meet your specific needs. Not "out of," but "according to" His riches. How rich is Christ? He's got it all, and that's available to you as you face your needs as husband and wife in your uncertain tomorrows.

This promise is built on the *personhood* of Jesus Christ, "in Christ Jesus." When Paul adds, "Christ Jesus," he brings us to heaven and brings glory down among us. The God up there becomes the God who is here. All that we need is ultimately in Christ. He is adequate! He will take the "cannots" out of your lives and replace them with "cans." In all of the things you must bear, you must do, you must meet—Christ Jesus will be your poise, your power, your plenty.

Because you are committed to Christ Jesus, believing His promises for all of your life, and because you desire to serve Him together through your marriage and home, it is my privilege to ask:

Who gives this woman to be married to this man?

(*Father or family member answers:* "*I do,*" "*We do,*" *or* "*Her mother and I do.*")

(*Minister then asks the couple to join hands and repeat their vows, the man being first:*)

I, _____(*man's name*), take thee _____ (*woman's name*) to be my wife in Christian marriage. I promise God and I promise you that I will be Christian in my actions and attitudes. I will serve the Lord with you; I will provide Christian leadership in our home. I will work to meet our financial responsibilities; I will be faithful to you and to you alone. I will weep with you in sorrow, rejoice with you in blessings, and be your faithful companion until Christ calls us home. I make this vow to you, so help me God.

(*The woman then repeats her vow to the man as the minister leads:*)

I, _____(*woman's name*), take thee _____ (*man's name*), to be my husband in the Lord. I promise God and I promise you that I will cherish you; I will obey you; I will love you; I will provide a shoulder to cry on, a heart that understands, a warm home for you to live in, and open arms for you to lean on. I will pray for you and encourage you; I will weep when you weep, laugh when you laugh, and be yours and yours alone until our

Lord separates us by death. This I solemnly and joyfully promise, so help me God.

Ring Service

Minister: To portray the exchanging of your marriage vows and as a public witness of them, you will now give these beautiful rings, symbolic of your promises.

(*Minister receives ring from ring bearer or best man and gives it to the groom, who places it on the third finger of the bride's left hand.*)

Minister: (*To the man*) Repeat after me and to _____(*woman's name*):

This ring is a picture of my love for you; I give it to you to wear in joy, I give it in humble gratitude that Christ led us together. In the name of the Father, the Son, and the Holy Spirit. Amen.

(*Minister receives ring from ring bearer, maid/matron of honor and gives it to the woman who places it on the third finger of the man's left hand.*)

Minister: (*To the man*) Repeat after me and to _____(*man's name*):

This ring is a picture of my love for you, I give it to you to wear with joy, I give it in humble gratitude that Christ led us together, In the name of the Father, the Son, and the Holy Spirit. Amen.

Pastoral prayer: (*Couple kneels or remains standing.*)

Pronouncement: Forasmuch as _____(*man's name*) and _____(*woman's name*) have promised God and one another that they will live together in the holy estate of matrimony, that they will be true to God and to each other, that they will build a life of mutual love and constant loyalty, in that they have witnessed the same with their vows and the giving of rings, it is my joy to pronounce that from this day forward in the sight of God and the laws of this state they are now husband and wife. May God bless you, and may you live together in holy love until life's end.

Recessional

14

Minister: (*To the congregation or assembled witnesses*)

Your presence here shows your love for _____(*woman's name*) and _____(*man's name*). You join this celebration because you affirm their union and want to bless their new relationship. You are saying to them that you are willing to share yourselves in loving friendship and that you will support them in time of need when they seek your help.

Prayer: Dear Lord, our Heavenly Father, we bless and thank You for the divine intention as given in the institution of marriage. Thank You for sustaining, strengthening, and supporting it in Your Word and by Your abiding presence in the hearts of those who love You and are willing to be obedient to You. We look to You, trust You, depend upon You to bless us with Your presence and care upon these two and all who have come together for this worship experience. In the name of our only Savior and reigning Lord we pray. Amen.

Minister: Believing that _____(*woman's name*) and _____(*man's name*) have truly sought and found the Lord's leadership and blessing in their desire to become one, it is my privilege to ask, "Who gives this woman to be married to this man?"

(*Father, family member, or friend gives the hand of the woman to the man or the minister and he continues*)

Minister's Charge: The eighth chapter of Romans is called by some the greatest of Paul's inspired writings. It highlights many great truths, but one inescapable truth keeps coming through: that life for a Christian is a life of grace. As you start life together, I want to offer some reminders and encouragement to you. I believe it will bless and assure you along the way.

Let me encourage you to remember that the life

of grace is a life of *no frustration*. God causes "all things to work together for good to those who love God, to those who are called according to his purpose" (*Rom. 8:28, NASB*). God makes all things to work together. This is the divine initiative in bringing about His purposes and will in your lives. Sometimes you may not understand your circumstances or events, but, remember, God's ways are not our ways. God's thoughts are not our thoughts. Keep the faith when you don't understand.

Remember also that the life of grace is a life of *no want*. "He who did not spare His own Son, but delivered Him up for us all, how will He not also with Him freely give us all things? (*Rom. 8:32*). David, hundreds of years before, phrased it this way: "The Lord is my shepherd; I shall not want" (*Ps. 23:1*). God knows your every need. Sometimes it is difficult for us to separate our wants from our needs. God has the wisdom to discern the difference. As you live obedient, God-honoring lives, the life of grace promises you will have no wants.

The life of grace is one of *no condemnation*

Who will bring a charge against God's elect? God is the one who justifies; who is the one who condemns? Christ Jesus is He who died, yes, rather who was raised, who is at the right hand of God, who also intercedes for us (Rom. 8:33-34).

The sin charge against man has been brought, but Christ met it and the believer is justified. There is now no condemnation. That does not mean that our conscience or Satan will not seek to reach into our memory and bring out past sins and wrongful actions and attitudes, but our Lord Jesus is praying in your behalf, and He will for as long as you live. That's amazing grace!

The life of grace is one of *no fear.*

Who shall separate us from the love of Christ? Shall tribulation, or distress, or persecution, or famine, or nakedness, or peril, or sword? . . . For I am convinced that neither death, nor life, nor angels, nor principalities, nor things present, nor things to come, nor powers, nor height, nor depth, nor any other created thing, shall be able to separate us from the love of God, which is in Christ Jesus our Lord (Rom. 8:35-39, NASB)

In your married life there will be those events, those anxious days, those uncertain hours, those circumstances which could place you in a world of fear, leaving you helpless and afraid. God's Word to you as you walk hand in hand through life is that when those clouds of fear appear, remember

you are secured forever in the love of God. An old
song says it this way:

> Safe in the arms of Jesus,
> Safe on His gentle breast,
> There by His love o'ershadowed,
> Sweetly my soul shall rest.

By His grace, you have come to this sacred
moment. _____(*man's name*), in taking this
woman whom you hold by the hand, do you
promise to love and cherish her, honor and keep
her, in sickness as in health, in poverty as in
wealth, for better or for worse, and be faithful to
_____(*woman's name*) so long as you both shall
live?
(*Man responds: "I do," or, "I will."*)
(*Minister continues:*) _____(*woman's name*), in
taking this man whom you hold by the hand, do
you promise to love and cherish him, to honor and
keep him, in sickness and in health, in poverty as
in wealth, for better, for worse, and be faithful to
_____(*man's name*) so long as you both shall
live?
(*Woman responds: "I do," or, "I will."*)
Minister: (*to the man*) Repeat this vow after me
and to your bride:

I accept you as my wife, with your strengths
and with your weaknesses; I will be loyal to you

in health or illness, to share what I have and who I am, to love enough to risk being hurt, to trust when I misunderstand, to weep with you in heartache, to celebrate life with you in joy, and I receive you as an equal in Christ, in the name of the Father, and of the Son, and of the Holy Spirit.

Minister: (*to the woman*) Repeat this vow after me and to your husband-to-be:

I accept you as my husband, with your strengths and with your weaknesses; I will be loyal to you in health or illness, to share what I have and who I am, to love enough to risk being hurt, to trust when I misunderstand, to weep with you in heartache, to celebrate life with you in joy, and I receive you as an equal in Christ, in the name of the Father, and of the Son, and of the Holy Spirit.

Ring Service

(*Minister receives ring from best man or ring bearer, hands it to the man who places it on the third finger of her left hand.*)

Minister: You will now exchange these beautiful rings with a vow that symbolizes your commitment to Christ and to each other in the vows you have just repeated:

(*Man repeats after the minister*)

I joyfully give you this wedding ring. It is a symbol of our united commitment. It is given reverently in the name of the Father, the Son, and the Holy Spirit. Amen.

(*Minister receives ring from maid/matron of honor or ring bearer and gives it to the woman who places it on the third finger of the man's left hand.*)

Woman: (*repeats after the minister*) I joyfully give you this wedding ring. It is a symbol of our united commitment. It is given reverently in the name of the Father, the Son, and the Holy Spirit. Amen.

Minister: (*or family member, or member of wedding party leads in prayer of dedication. The couple may stand or kneel.*)

The Declaration of Marriage: Forasmuch as _____(*man's name*) and _____(*woman's name*) have promised God and each other that they have committed themselves to a Christian marriage and home, the noblest and best relationship between a man and a woman, the most cherished and personal of all human relationships, it is my privileged honor as a minister of the gospel of Christ, the gospel of grace, and in the authority vested in me by the laws of this state, I pronounce you husband and wife. May God bless your union. (*Kiss is optional. Couple faces congregation and the minister introduces:*)

I am happy to introduce Mr. and Mrs. _____.

Recessional

15

Minister: (*Statement of Marriage:*)

A wedding is obviously not the occasion for a long and detailed sermon. All the excitement that has surrounded this day, the plans, the preparation, the thrill, and expectancy of this moment itself make me quite sure that if you are to remember anything at all now it will have to be the simplest thing! So let me give you a text, one that sums up in itself all that I really want to say to you today. It is Leviticus 6:13, and this is how it reads: "The fire shall ever be burning upon the altar; it shall never go out." And I just want to point out three things about it.

It Describes a Practice

This passage, from verses 8 to 13, describes the law of the burnt offering given by the Lord to Moses and the people of God. It describes part of the worship of God's people in Old Testament times, the bringing of sacrifices and offerings to the Lord and the presenting of them upon the altar as the expression of their repentance, love, and devotion to Him—the "figure" which, as Hebrews

9:9-15 tells us, the Lord Jesus came to fulfill as He "offered himself without spot to God" (*v. 11*).

So upon this special altar at which the people worshiped and consecrated themselves to God, a flame burned night and day. "The fire shall ever be burning upon the altar; it shall never go out." So the first thing we must say about this verse is that, as a historical fact, it describes a practice. But much more is important for us here today:

It Suggests a Picture

For instance, how that steadily burning flame, never going out, expresses our longing for the love that burns between your two hearts today! Without becoming too sentimental, it is surely nevertheless true that the love of your hearts burns very brightly together today. And this verse applied in this way expresses our longing for your love for each other. But much more! It expresses our longing for your love for the Lord. Charles Wesley, in one of his greatest hymns, put it like this: "Kindle a flame of sacred love, on the mean altar of my heart. There let it for Thy glory burn, with inextinguishable blaze."

Now, we rejoice that this is a Christian marriage today, and that individually the miracle of new birth has happened in your hearts; but now as you seek to bring all the future to Him, your hearts, your lives and your home, let this be true: "The flame shall ever be burning upon the altar." "There let it for Thy glory burn, with inextinguishable blaze!" And that brings me to the third thing about this verse:

It Reveals a Principle

The flame did not burn untended and uncared for, but it had to be cared for and fed. The passage tells us how. Each day (*v. 11*), the old ashes had to be cleared away. Each day (*v. 12*), new fuel had to be added to it, and only as that was done could the offering rise to God every day. The flame had to be tended; it was not by accident that it burned.

So it will be with your marriage. Take time to tend the flame. Do not let business commitments and ambitions or anything else cause you to neglect each other. Remove the ashes each day; never let the sun go down upon your anger. Renew the flame with something every day. How many marriages have grown utterly cold because the couple did not take time to tend the flame!

And so it will be with your love to God. Take time to tend the flame there—every day! How busy we can get today. With the two of you at business—either genuinely to make ends meet or perhaps to provide those things for the home that were once luxuries but are now seemingly necessities—the flame of love for God can be so easily neglected, and the Lord's Day can become the lazy day, or a day to go chasing all over the countryside, "relaxing" and seeing friends.

Tend the flame! God will not let the flame die, but you can neglect it till it becomes but a travesty of what it ought to be. Thank God, His love for us, for you, and for me, has never died! It is "steadfast love," love that went "all the way to Calvary," "love to the loveless shown that they might lovely be!" And, thank God, He does not quench the "smoking flax" (*Matt. 12:20*). But let us make absolutely sure that from our side it is tended. Tend the flame! Let Charles Wesley's words be your prayer, for today and for every day:

Jesus, confirm my heart's desire
    To work and speak and think for Thee;
Still let me guard the holy fire,
    And still stir up Thy gift in me.

Minister: After prayer, counsel, and meditation you have reached this decisive crossroads in your life. Because you believe it is God's will for you to be one in Christ, to serve Him together in your home and through His church, and to demonstrate His love through your union, it is my privilege to ask, Who gives this woman to be married to this man?

(*Father, family member or friend responds with, "I do," "We do," "Her mother and I do," or a statement to the couple and assembled witnesses before he gives the hand of the woman to the man.*)

Minister: I will ask you to join hands, face each other, and repeat your vows of commitment:

"I, _____(*man's name*), take you, _____ (*woman's name*), as my wedded wife, though the unknown future bring joy or sorrow, health or sickness, prosperity or adversity, sunshine or shadow, hopes fulfilled or dreams shattered, I pledge to be true to you for the rest of my life."

(*Woman repeats her vow to the man following the minister's lead:*)

I, _____(*woman's name*), take you, _____(*man's name*), as my wedded husband, though the unknown future bring joy or sorrow, health or sickness, prosperity or adversity, sunshine or shadow, hopes fulfilled or dreams shattered, I pledge to be true to you, for the rest of my life.

Ring Service: (*Minister receives the ring from best man or ring bearer, gives it to the man, who places it on the third finger of the woman's left hand.*) (*Man: repeating after the minister:*)

_____(*woman's name*), I give you this ring as a symbol of my commitment to you, and as a token of my conviction that the Lord in His perfect will has brought us together. In the name of the Father, and of the Son, and of the Holy Spirit. (*Minister receives the ring from maid/matron of honor or ring bearer, gives it to the woman who places it on the third finger of the man's left hand.*)

_____(*man's name*), I give this ring to you as a symbol of my commitment to you, and as a token of my conviction that the Lord in His perfect will has brought us together. In the name of the Father, and of the Son, and of the Holy Spirit. **Prayer:** (*Minister, friend, family member can lead in this while couple stands or kneels.*)

Dear Father: As our Lord God Almighty, we ask You to send Your light and truth upon _____(*man's name*) and _____(*woman's name*) all the days of their lives. Lord, by Your hand protect them. Father, with Your eye guide them. If it be Thy will, bestow upon them the gift and heritage of children and help them to see them brought up in the ways of the Lord. May You be glorified through this new home. In Jesus' name, Amen.

MINISTER: Forasmuch as you, _____(*woman's name*), and you, _____(*man's name*), have pledged your vows and exchanged rings symbolic of your lifelong commitments to a Christian marriage and home, you have promised to encourage each other in a spiritual walk, and to assist each other in being all that Christ wants you to be, it is my happy privilege to pronounce that from this day forward, you are now husband and wife.

I am happy to introduce to you Mr. and Mrs. _____.

(*Couple may kiss, bride receives her flowers, and recessional begins.*)

16

(*Minister opens the service with prayer.*)

Minister: Dearly Beloved: The most important step in a person's life other than his coming to Jesus Christ as Savior and Lord is the decision to link that life to another in marriage. Many people come to marriage with high expectations, but wrong expectations. True love and true marriage is a lifetime of giving, for love is something you do.

Marriage is an empty box. There's nothing in it. It is an opportunity to put something in, to do something for marriage. Marriage was never intended to do anything for anybody; people are expected to do something for marriage. Love isn't in marriage, it is in people, and people put love into marriage.—J. Allan Peterson, *The Myth of the Greener Grass.*

Marriage then takes on a certain amount of maturity and understanding that it is more than an event or an emotion, it is the giving of one's self to another for their highest and best welfare. Therefore, it should not be entered into unadvisedly or lightly, but discreetly, soberly, and in the guidance and counsel of the Holy Spirit.

Believing you understand this, I ask you, _____(*man's name*), do you promise in the presence of God and this gathering of family and friends to seek to be all Christ wants you to be, to encourage your wife in her spiritual walk, to practice love as a giver more than a getter, to dedicate your home and the raising of any children the Lord may give you to the glory of God, and do you commit your best in making every part of your life together to be pleasing and honoring to the Lord? Do you so promise?

(Man responds: "I promise," "I do," or "I will. Minister then addresses the woman:)

_____(*woman's name*), do you promise in the presence of God and this gathering of family and friends, to seek to be all Christ wants you to be, to encourage your husband in his spiritual walk, to practice love as a giver more than a getter, to dedicate your home and the raising of any children the Lord may give you to the glory of God, and do you commit your best in making every part of your life together to be pleasing and honoring to the Lord? Do you so promise?

*(Woman responds, "I promise," "I do," or "I will."
Minister then addresses the father, friend, or family member who is to give the woman away:)*

Minister: Who gives this woman to be married to this man?

*(Father, friend, or family member responds "I do,"
"We do," or "Her mother and I do." He then joins the hands of the couple together and is seated.)*

(Minister addresses the couple.)

Minister: _____*(man's name)* and _____ *(woman's name)*, in Genesis 2:7-9,15,18,21-23 *(NIV)* we read these words:

> And the Lord God formed man from the dust of the ground and breathed into his nostrils the breath of life, and man became a living being.
>
> Now the Lord God had planted a garden in the east, in Eden; and there he put the man he had formed. And the Lord God made all kinds of trees grow out of the ground—trees that were pleasing to the eye and good for food.
>
> The Lord God took the man and put him in the Garden of Eden to work it and take care of it.
>
> The Lord God said, "It is not good for the man to be alone. I will make a helper suitable for him."
>
> So the Lord God caused the man to fall into a deep sleep; and while he was sleeping, he took one of the man's ribs and closed up the place with flesh.

Then the Lord God made a woman from the
rib he had taken out of the man, and he brought
her to the man.

The man said,

> "This is now bone of my bones,
>   and flesh of my flesh;
> she shall be called 'woman,'
>   for she was taken out of man."

Marriage is a need-meeting relationship. It was
so during your courtship and continues till the last
day a couple is together. No one is so unselfish
that he marries with a pure desire to meet someone else's need and asks nothing for himself.
Wanting our needs to be met is neither sinful nor
selfish. It has been said that love is the accurate
estimate and supply of another's needs.

Adam and Eve, though perfect and innocent,
had various kinds of needs. God created them that
way. They had social, emotional, physical, and
spiritual needs, and this was before their fall into
sin. In fact, their fall was actually the attempt to
satisfy those needs in a way and at a time contrary
to the plan of the Creator.

God put man with his needs in a position
where his needs could be met. He was placed in
a beautiful garden and was told to cultivate it,
keep it, and eat from it. His needs for beauty,
work, food could be satisfied from his surround-
ings. He was not left alone but was given another

person and told to share, unite, procreate. His needs for companionship, intimacy, continuity, and family would be met through other people. He was given fellowship with God. His needs for ultimate meaning, purpose, and eternal life would be met by God alone. Only certain needs can be met in marriage by another person. Not all. But the essence of the marriage promise is, "I will meet these needs."

The wedding vows say it: "to have and to hold" —commitment; "For better, for worse"—belonging; "For richer, for poorer"—loyalty; "In sickness and in health"—support; "To love and to cherish"—faithfulness; "Til death do us part"— companionship. That is a tall order! No wonder we all sometimes fail. I'm not suggesting we dilute the vows, but rather that we understand how they are translated and applied to our partner's everyday needs. The needs of two people seldom dovetail perfectly, but when each partner is seriously seeking to meet the needs of the other, the problem of a third party has little opportunity to develop.—Peterson, pg. 51-53, *The Myth of Greener Grass.*

Each partner has five basic needs: attention, acceptance, affection, admiration, and activities. God has led you together to fill those needs in each other. Therefore, I ask you to join hands, face each other, and make your vow to meet these needs

God has placed within you, to His glory and the fulfilling of your life.

(*Minister asks the man to repeat after him this vow:*)

I, _____(*man's name*), take thee, _____ (*woman's name*), to be my wedded wife, to have and to hold, from this day forward, for better, for worse, for richer, for poorer, in sickness and in health, to love and to cherish, till death us do part according to God's holy ordinance, and thereto I plight thee my troth.

(*The woman shall repeat after the minister:*)

I, _____(*woman's name*), take thee, _____(*man's name*), to be my wedded husband, to have and to hold, from this day forward, for better, for worse, for richer, for poorer, in sickness and in health, to love and to cherish, and to obey, till death us do part, according to God's holy ordinance, and thereto I plight thee my troth.

(*They loose their hands, the minister takes the rings from best man, maid/matron of honor or ring bearer, and holding them up says:*)

These rings are the symbols of the vows here taken; circles of wholeness, perfect in form. These rings mark the beginning of your long journey together, filled with wonder, surprises, laughter, tears, celebration, grief, and joy. May these rings glow in reflection of the warmth and the love which flow through the wearers today.

(The minister gives the ring to the man, who places it upon the third finger of the woman's left hand. Holding the ring there, he repeats after the minister:)

In token and pledge of the vow between us made, with this ring I thee wed, and with all my worldly goods I thee endow, in the name of the Father, and of the Son, and of the Holy Spirit. Amen.

(The minister gives the ring to the woman who places it on the third finger of the man's left hand. Holding the ring there, she repeats after the minister:)

In token and pledge of the vow between us made, with this ring I thee wed, and with all my worldly goods I thee endow, in the name of the Father, and of the Son, and of the Holy Spirit. Amen.

(Then the minister leads in prayer. The couple may kneel or stand.)

Dear Heavenly Father, Creator and Preserver of all persons, the Giver and Author of eternal life, may your gracious blessings rest upon this man and this woman. Give them the will and heart to do and keep their vows; let this covenant never be broken by the sin of neglect, or the transgression of infidelity. May their home be a place of blessing and a tower of strength, and may they live peacefully, joyfully, and in this covenant until You call them home. In the peerless name of Jesus Christ our Lord we pray. Amen.

(*The couple joins hands and stands before the minister. He puts his hands on theirs and says:*)

You have given and exchanged your vows and your rings. Believing the ideals and the commitments you both have made to be in accord with God's holy will, and believing that they are binding for as long as you live, and believing you will keep them inviolate because they are true and based on God's plan for people, it is my privilege as a minister of the gospel to pronounce you husband and wife, in the name of the Father, and of the Son, and of the Holy Spirit. Amen.

I am happy to introduce to you Mr. and Mrs. _____.

Recessional

17

Minister: (*To assembled witnesses*)

Dear family, friends, and honored man and woman, God has unusual ways of laying His hands upon His loved ones. He loved us in creation; He prepares a place for us in heaven that we can share eternity with him; He calls us home in His sovereignty and to Himself in death. In His loving care He gives us the joy of union with another of His children in the divine institution we call marriage.

Marriage was created, is strengthened, upheld, and sustained by his grace and love. I charge you who witness this union today to see it as a part of God's work as Shepherd and Guardian of His people, and I charge you who come to be joined _____ and _____ *(man's and woman's names)* to remember that the love of God is sufficient to sustain you through all the years ahead as you obey His principles as maturing Christians.

_____*(man's name)*, will you have _____*(woman's name)* to be your wedded wife? Will you covenant to love her in the midst of the everydayness of life? Will you share with her the responsibility of building a Christian home, and will you seek to join diligently with her in following God's will for your life?

(Man answers: "I do," or "I will." Minister faces the woman and asks:)

Will you, _____*(woman's name)*, have _____*(man's name)* to be your wedded husband? Will you covenant to love him in the midst of the everydayness of life? Will you share with him the responsibility of building a Christian home, and will you seek to join diligently with him in following God's will for your life?

(*Woman answers: "I do," or "I will."*)

(*Minister then asks:*) Who gives this woman to be married to this man?

(*Father, family member, or friend responds with "I do," "We do," or "Her mother and I do," and joins the hands of the man and woman together and is seated.*)

Minister: Before you receive one another, I want to bring you a challenge and a reminder from God's Word. Proverbs 24:3-4 states: "By wisdom a house is built, And by understanding it is established; and by knowledge the rooms are filled With all precious and pleasant riches" (*NASB*).

The Bible speaks often of house and home. Jesus spoke of salvation as entering your house today when he dealt with Zaccheus. Paul spoke of the conversion of the household of the Philippian jailer when he said, "You and your house shall be saved." Joshua related his commitment to following the Lord with his entire family when he stated: "As for me and my house, we will serve the Lord."

The home becomes a picture for eternity when the promise is made in Revelation 21:3: "Now the dwelling of God is with men, and he will live with them" (*NIV*). As you begin your home building, remember that God is the Architect; you are the builders. How do you build a home on the rock—one that will stand the test of time, storm, and adversity?

You start with a firm *foundation*. It takes God to make a marriage. The Greek word for home is "the shrine of the gods." Your home, because of your personal relationship to Jesus Christ, will not be a "shrine of the gods" but the abiding place of the one true God. Every person ought to have three homes: a church home, a family home, a heavenly home. That is a great and firm foundation. With Christ as the foundation of your home, you can build a home that will last as long as you do.

You will continue building your home by raising good *walls* of communication. Most marriages that end in trouble do so, not because of blowouts but slow leaks. Many active marriage counselors consider the failure of proper communication between husband and wife to be a major cause of family problems. Let me urge you to take time for communication. Take time to understand your partner. Take time to speak in love. Take time to be a good listener. Take time to unconditionally accept your mate, even as you discover frailties and weaknesses. Rejection is one of the greatest fears of persons. Communication means acceptance. Build strong walls of communication.

You complete your house by adding the *roof* of commitment. A commitment so strong that separation is not even an option. Someone has said that wars are not won by evacuation. Neither are homes built in isolation. Whatever happens to shake your love, remember you have a commitment. Love is a promise more than a feeling. It is an activity directed toward another person. It is a conscious act of the will. James reminded us that faith was something that showed up in activity. Love is a choice. It is an action more than a reaction. As you make your commitment with this kind of understanding, you remove cheap sentimentality and put reality, effort, and discipline into your developing life and love.

Thus, with the firm foundation of God at the very heart of your home, the walls of communication, and the roof of commitment—that is wisdom. As Solomon said, "A house is built."

Believing you desire this kind of home, are you ready to receive one another as a gift from God and exchange your vows of commitment?
(*Couple answers, "We are."*)
Groom's vows:

_____(*woman's name*), I leave my father and mother and commit all that I am to you. By God's Spirit and day-by-day choosing, I will love you as Jesus loves His church. This means that I will sacrificially lay down my rights and my life for you. I will continue to die to my individuality, likes, preferences, ideas, opinions, and plans as a single man. For we shall be one.

I will provide for you and protect you from pressures and dangers and in areas of weaknesses by setting boundaries for you.

As head I will provide loving leadership and be priest and prophet—going before God on your behalf and speaking forth what God tells me.

I will also choose to love you as I love my own body, recognizing that you are my partner in marriage and that we are heirs together of the grace of life.

I shall let you in on my troubles and problems, so we may face them together.

I will live with you in an understanding way, always seeking to make certain that my ways of showing you love are the ways you need to be loved.

I will honor you, be faithful to you, and cherish you as long as we both live.

Bride's Vows:

_____(*man's name*), I will leave my father and mother and cleave to you. I will become one with you. I will be submissive to you in the fear of the Lord, out of my love, respect, and total trust in you. I will depend totally on the Lord Jesus

Christ and His Holy Spirit to work these things out and to fill me with all the love I need to be your completion, your wife.

I will support and uplift you by word and deed by putting more emphasis on what you are than what you aren't.

I will seek to respond to you in love as I would to Jesus Himself. I will comfort and encourage you, pray for you, and challenge you. I will strive to keep our communication open and honest and trust God to give me a humble and forgiving heart.

I desire to be a crown to your head and bring honor to your name.

I will cherish you as God's gift to me, whose value is immeasurable.

Exchange of Rings:

(*Minister receives the rings from the best man, maid/matron of honor or ring bearer, and states:*)

The rings which you will place on the finger of your loved one was fashioned in a circle which does not end, signifying the quality of your marriage, a love that has a sense of eternity in it. This public symbol of your love and commitment to each other shall be a sign of joy.

_____(*man's name*), will you take this ring and place it on _____'s(*woman's name*) hand and repeat these words after me?

With this ring I thee wed, and with it I give thee my love and devotion. In the name of the Father, and of the Son, and of the Holy Spirit. Amen.

_____(*woman's name*), will you take this ring and place it on _____'s(*man's name*) hand and repeat these words after me?

With this ring I thee wed, and with it I give thee my love and devotion. In the name of the Father and of the Son, and of the Holy Spirit. Amen.

Minister: Would you join me in prayer?

(*Couple kneels or stands and the minister places his hands on theirs as he prays. After the prayer, the couple stands and faces the minister who says:*)

And now, in recognition of the vows you have uttered, the commitment you have made to building a Christ-honoring home, in accordance with the laws of this state, and as an ordained minister of the gospel of Jesus Christ, it gives me the greatest of pleasure to pronounce you husband and wife, Mrs. and Mrs. _____; and may God richly bless you.

(*Bride receives her bouquet, and the couple leads the recessional.*)

18

(*Ceremony conducted for my daughter, Jane Elizabeth (Betsy), and her husband, Daniel De Armas.*)

Minister:

Dearly Beloved: We are gathered together in this house of worship, before the presence of God and these assembled witnesses to join together this man and this woman in the holy estate of matrimony. Marriage is commended by God to be an honorable institution, for it is that human relationship that God has chosen to be symbolic of the relationship of Jesus Christ to His bride, the church.

_____ (*man's name*) and _____ _____ (*woman's name*), you have made the most important decision in your life, to trust Jesus Christ as your personal Savior and Lord. You have grown in Him and He has directed you in your lives and now to each other and made this day a reality. You know this to be God's will for your lives. You have sought the leadership of the Holy Spirit in this matter and also the counsel of others the Lord has placed in your lives as your spiritual authorities—your parents. You come to this day having those principles in God's Word which have been instilled in you throughout your lives to guide you in this important and blessed event in your spiritual pilgrimage. Because marriage is a covenant between each of you and to God, I want to ask you the following questions:

_____ (*man's name*), because you are to

be the spiritual leader in your home, do you have this woman to be your wedded wife, to live together according to the ordinance of God in the holy estate of marriage? Do you promise to honor, keep, and comfort her—in sickness and in health, in prosperity and adversity, and forsaking all others, keep thee only unto her so long as you both shall live?

(Groom answers: "I do," or "I will.")

_____ *(woman's name)*, do you have this man to be your wedded husband, to live together after God's ordinance in the holy estate of matrimony? Do you promise to love him, honor him, serve him, and keep him in sickness and in health, in prosperity and adversity, and keep thee only unto him so long as you both shall live?

(Bride answers: "I do," or "I will.")

Minister: Because of your commitment to God and to each other, it then becomes my privilege and responsibility to inquire: Who gives this woman to be married to this man?

(Father responds: "I do," "We do," or "Her mother and I do," or as an option, the response I used when giving our daughter, Betsy in marriage: "Her mother and I do.")

In so doing, we would like to welcome you, *(man's name)*, into our family. We are pleased to be a part of your family. In just a few moments I am going to lower the veil over (*woman's name*) face. That will be symbolic of her passing from our basic spiritual responsibility and care to yours. (*Mother's name*) and I have been her spiritual leaders for (*number*) years. In a few minutes, she will become your spiritual responsibility. We trust you. We believe that which we have started, you will continue. It is a privilege to entrust our (*daughter's name*) to you to be her husband and her spiritual leader for the years to come.

(*Daughter's name*), you have been such a joy to your mother and father for these (*number*) years. We prayed for you, and when we knew you were conceived we asked God to give us a healthy child, and He did. Then we asked the Lord to save you. The Lord granted our request and you accepted Jesus Christ as your personal Savior and as your Lord.

We prayed for you to be under His lordship—that wherever He led, you would follow Him, and you made that commitment. God granted that request. Then we asked the Lord to make you pure and chaste, and the Lord granted our request. Then we prayed that you would be obedient to your parents, to our spiritual leadership, and you were. The Lord granted our request.

Finally, we prayed that there would be a man somewhere that He was raising to be your spiritual leader, a man to love you and be a strength to you. The Lord granted our request and sent (*man's name*). Your mother and father love you very much. We have complete confidence in (*man's name*) to pick up these obligations and responsibilities. We have raised you that way, and the time has come for the transfer of spiritual and material responsibility.

We thank you for (*number*) beautiful, wonderful years. You are something special to us and you always will be. Now, as I lower the veil, (*lower veil*) and as (*man's name*) raises it at the conclusion of this service, you will be under his spiritual leadership and his spiritual obligation for the rest of your life. God bless you.

(*Minister joins the hand of the bride and groom together.*)

In Ecclesiastes 4:12, God's Word has a powerful truth. "A cord of three strands is not quickly torn apart" (*NASB*). This is similar to our saying, "In unity there is strength." Just as three strands woven together are stronger than a single strand, it is also true that people together in certain situations are more effective than if they go their separate ways. As you two become one, let me urge you to make a cord of three strands.

The first strand is the strand of your personal commitment to Jesus Christ. "Jesus is Lord" is not a trite expression but a declaration for life and eternity. The first commandment has never changed. "You shall have no other gods before Me" (Ex. 20:3, *NASB*). Jesus followed that up with, "And you shall love the Lord your God with all your heart, and with all your soul, and with all your mind, and with all your strength" (Mark 12:30, *NASB*).

As much as you tenderly cherish each other, your relationship must derive its love, strength, and beauty from your basic and prior relationship to Jesus Christ. Prayer, Bible study and meditation will foster your spiritual growth, and this first strand will be the heart of this powerful cord.

The second strand is your developing life together—your home and marriage. A person living only for himself is incomplete and unfulfilled. Adam, who had a perfect environment was still conscious of a missing element in his life. God inaugurated the home and marriage in the Garden of Eden. His desire is that two people under His leadership can respond to one another with understanding and love.

Your home should bring you spiritual, emotional, and physical fulfillment. The home where love reigns is more like heaven than any other place in today's world. Your home becomes a castle, a refuge, a place of renewal. Protect it. Build it.

Sanctify it. Let its walls reverberate with joy and happy laughter. Let it be a cool spring in a hot day. May it comfort you in your sorrows and be a caress for your cares. Let it be, next to God, your strongest bond.

The third strand of the cord not easily broken is your service to Christ through His body, the church. The new Testament puts much importance on the fellowship of the saints. The apostle John emphasized the fact that believers in Christ are a part of a forever family in a deep, personal relationship and responsibility to one another. Paul called the church the body of Christ. Peter spoke of believers as living stones built into a spiritual house.

For your welfare and to be obedient to Christ, you will not try to stand alone and apart from the Lord's church but will give your best by being active in that expression of His body. In so doing, you will share in God's ultimate purpose for the world; you will see God at work in the fabric of everyday people, the salvation of the lost, the up-building of homes, the victory of celebration, the quiet strength of togetherness. The rewards will be many, but the greatest will be His words at the end of the day, "Well done, good and faithful servants."

The Cord of Three Strands: The Lord Jesus,

your home, your church and her ministries. These compose a cord that "is not quickly torn apart."

The Vows

I, _____ (*man's name*), take thee, _____ (*woman's name*) to my Christian wife, to have and to hold from this day forward, for better for worse, for richer for poorer, in sickness and in health, to love and to cherish, till death do us part according to God's holy ordinance; and thereto I give thee my troth.

I, _____ (*woman's name*), take thee _____ (*man's name*), to my Christian husband, to have and to hold from this day forward, for better for worse, for richer for poorer, in sickness and in health, to love, to cherish and to obey, till death do us part, according to God's holy ordinance; and thereto I give thee my troth.

Ring Vows: (*man's name*) and (*woman's name*), from time immemorial the ring has been used for important covenants. When the race was young and parliamentary government was not yet in existence, the reigning monarch would place a seal on the ring and with that seal they would authenticate their royal edicts. That seal became a sign or the only token of imperial authority.

Through the years, friends have exchanged a

band of gold to evidence a friendship which is true and enduring.

When we come to the marital altar, this ring takes on a meaning even more beautiful. Here it represents a love that, as the ring, has no beginning nor end. And as it is made of gold it signifies that there are no impurities in it—that it is a pure and Christian love.

*This ring, particularly, has even a more significant meaning because it has been in your family, (*man's name*), since (*relative*), and later your own dear (*relative*), and now you are going to give it to (*woman's name*) (who you are making your bride). So this ring represents a Christian tradition and a total surrender to the things of God.

(*This section may be adapted or eliminated.*)

Place this ring on (*woman's name*) finger and repeat after me:

"I give you this ring as a symbol of my love for you and make you my partner of the material goods that God has given me and of those which He might give me in the future."

(*Woman's name*), this ring that you're giving to (*man's name*) will be something he'll always be proud of, and wear with memories of this day and of the vows he made to the Lord and to you. And (*man's name*), as you wear this ring given with all the love of a young lady's heart, I hope you will always be proud of it. (*Woman's name*), I know that you're giving it as a symbol of your love for (*man's name*) and your commitment to Jesus Christ. May you cherish it, (*man's name*), and wear it until the day Jesus calls you home.

(*Woman's name*), if you will place the ring on (*man's name*) finger and repeat after me and to (*man's name*) this vow: "With this ring, I thee wed, and with all my worldly goods, and my heart's affection I thee endow, in the name of the Father, and the Son, and the Holy Spirit. Amen."

Prayer: Our Heavenly Father, Your love is always hovering over those that serve You and honor You. Father, we thank You because (*woman's name*) and (*man's name*) have decided to unite their lives in service to You asking for the prayers of their parents, the guidance of their pastors, and the support of their churches.

I ask you, Father, to honor that request and this wish: that You give them victory in their lives. That everything they might try in Your name might be successful. That it might be a success according to Your standards and not the way we measure it.

We ask, Father, that in the days of sadness You might be their comforter, in the days of happiness You will also be He who listens and rejoices with them.

Father, we pray that when their children come You might give them obedient children, children who will honor You and who might be their joy and pride.

And Father, let the words that have been said here and the feelings which have been expressed become a part of the lives of (*woman's name*) and (*man's name*) from now and forevermore. In the name of Christ Jesus. Amen.

Forasmuch as you, (*man's name*), _____ and you, _____ (*woman's name*), have consented together in holy wedlock and have witnessed the same before God and this company by pledging your vows each to the other, you've declared it by the giving of rings and by the joining of hands, it is my privilege to pronounce that from this moment on, in the sight of heaven and earth you are now husband and wife. May God's grace and peace be forever upon you.

_____ (*man's name*), you may kiss your bride.

On behalf of the _____'s and the _____'s (*family name of man and family name of woman*) and the fellowship of faith, I am happy to introduce to you, Mr. and Mrs. _____.

Suggested Candle Ceremony

VOWS

Groom: _____(*woman's name*), God has been faithfully building us in a growing love. The foundation of this love is not human affection alone but a strong recognition that God has called us to Himself and to each other.

Therefore, my beloved, I promise both you and our Heavenly Father that by the power of the Holy Spirit I will love you as Christ loved the church, denying myself and considering you more important.

I desire to be your spiritual leader, counselor, provider, protector, lover, and friend—always using the Bible as my authority. I love you; please be my wife.

Bride: _____(*man's name*), Jesus Christ calls us to be His bride. The Bible teaches us to recognize God's authority and be submissive to it. Today, I acknowledge that God has placed you in authority over me. As the Holy Spirit controls and empowers me, I will fit in with your plans. I will respect you. I will build you up as a man. I will encourage and challenge you in your walk toward maturity in Christ, so our lives and our home will bring honor and glory to God. Yes, I will be your wife.

Candle Ceremony

(*Minister explains the symbolism and lighting of the candles:*)

The yellow candle is given by the bride's mother, symbolizing the radiance of Christ's love. The green candle is given by the groom's mother, symbolizing the growth of Christ in their lives. The center white candle symbolizes Christ in His holiness, with the yellow and green molded around the white.

The two outside candles have been lit by your mothers, representing your lives to this moment. They are two distinct lights, each capable of going their own separate ways. To bring joy and harmony to your home, there must be the merging of these two lights into one. This is what the Lord meant when He said, "For this reason a man shall leave his father and mother and be joined to his wife, and the two shall become one flesh" (*Matt 19:5, RSV*).

From now on your thoughts shall be for each other rather than your individual selves. Your plans shall be mutual; your joys and sorrows shall be shared alike.

_____(*woman's name*) and _____(*man's name*) will light the molded candle expressing the goal of their union: to grow in Christ and radiate

His love to all whose lives they touch. They do not extinguish their candles, but instead place them back in their original places still lit, symbolizing that their individual personalities remain, yet from this day forward, by God, are merged together as one.

(*Bride and Groom Go to Candle Table and Solo Begins.*)

A Ceremony Involving Parents

(*Minister speaks to both sets of parents:*)

Would Mr. and Mrs. _____, (*bride's parents*) and Mr. and Mrs. _____ (*groom's parents*) please stand?

It is traditional for the father of the bride to give her away. However, in a real sense, both sets of parents share in the giving and receiving. It is the joining of two families. Therefore, Mr. and Mrs. _____, (*groom's parents*) do you not only give your son, _____ (*man's name*) to be _____'s (*woman's name*) husband, but also joyfully receive _____ (*woman's name*) as your daughter?"

(*Parents respond: "We do."*)

Mr. and Mrs. _____ (*bride's parents*), do you not only joyfully give your daughter, _____ (*woman's name*) to _____ (*man's name*) as his wife, but receive _____ (*man's name*) to be your son?"

(Parents respond: "We do.")
Minister: Who gives this woman to be married to this man?
(Father lifts veil and kisses bride.)

Acknowledgments

For material on pp. 24-32 of this book: to Agape Ministries for use of Wedding Vows, Rehearsal Information, and The Wedding Ceremony from *Planning a Christ-centered Wedding* © 1979 by Agape Ministries, Titusville, FL. Used by permission.

For quotation on p. 161: to Tyndale House Publishers, Inc. from *The Myth of the Greener Grass* by J. Allan Petersen. Published by Tyndale House Publishers, Inc., © 1983 by J. Allan Petersen. Used by permission.

For the Suggested Candle Ceremony on pp. 183-185: to Fleming H. Revell Company. From *The Christian Wedding Handbook* by Kay Oliver Lewis Copyright © 1981 by Kay Oliver Lewis. Published by Fleming H. Revell Company. Used by permission.

For a Ceremony Involving Parents on p. 186: to Harvest House Publishers taken from *How Can I Be Sure?* by Bob Phillips, copyright 1978, Harvest House Publishers, 1075 Arrowsmith, Eugene, OR 97402. Used by permission.